Rick Steves'

TRAVEL
AS A
POLITICAL
ACT

NATION
BOOKS
New York

Credits:
Europe Through the Back Door Lead Editor: Cameron Hewitt
ETBD Managing Editor: Risa Laib
ETBD Proofreader: Lauren Mills
Nation Proofreader: Jeff Georgeson
Interior Design and Layout: Rhonda Pelikan
Graphics: Rhonda Pelikan, Barb Geisler, Laura VanDeventer
Photography: Rick Steves, Cameron Hewitt, Dominic Bonuccelli,
Abdi Sami, Steve Smith, Anthony P. Lilly, Bill Adams

Published by Nation Books, A Member of the Perseus Books Group
116 East 16th Street, 8th Floor
New York, NY 10003

Nation Books is a co-publishing venture of the Nation Institute
and the Perseus Books Group

Books published by Nation Books are available at special discounts for bulk
purchases in the United States by corporations, institutions, and other
organizations. For more information, please contact the Special Markets
Department at the Perseus Books Group, 2300 Chestnut Street, Suite 200,
Philadelphia, PA 19103, or call (800) 810-4145, ext. 5000,
or e-mail special.markets@perseusbooks.com.

A CIP catalog record for this book is available from the Library of Congress.
LCCN: 2009922566
ISBN-13: 978-1-56858-435-5

10 9 8 7 6 5 4 3 2

Contents

Introduction

O n a visit to Turkey, I met a dervish. Dervishes—who are sort of like Muslim monks—follow Rumi, a mystic poet and philosopher of divine love. (I like to think Rumi and St. Francis would hit it off well.) They're called "whirling dervishes" because they spin in a circle as they pray. The dervish allowed me to observe his ritual on the condition that I understood what it meant to him.

The dervish led me to his flat rooftop—a peaceful oasis in the noisy city of Konya—where he prayed five times a day. With the sun heavy and red on the horizon, he explained, "When we pray, we keep one foot in our community, anchored in our home. The other foot steps around and around like this, acknowledging the beautiful variety of God's creation…touching all corners of this great world. I raise one hand up to acknowledge the love of God, and the other hand goes down like the spout of a teapot. As I spin around, my hand above receives the love from our Creator, and my hand below showers it onto all of his creation."

As the dervish whirled and whirled, he settled into a meditative trance. And so did I. Watching his robe billow out and his head tilt over, I saw a conduit of love acknowledging the greatness of God. This man was so different from me, yet actually very much the same. This chance interaction left me with a renewed appreciation of the rich diversity of humanity…as well as its fundamental oneness.

Experiences like this one can be any trip's most treasured souvenir. When we return home, we can put what we've learned— our newly acquired broader perspective—to work as citizens of a great nation confronted with unprecedented challenges. And when we do that, we make travel a political act.

I enjoyed my most powerful travel experience ever on my first trip overseas. I was a 14-year-old with my parents, visiting relatives in Norway. We were in Oslo's vast Frogner Park—which, then as now, is filled with Gustav Vigeland's great stony statues of humans of all ages, shapes, and sizes.

Immersed in this grand, chiseled celebration of family and humanity, I gained a new insight into my little world. I noticed how much my parents were loving me. Their world revolved around me. They would do anything to make me happy and help me enjoy a fulfilling life. At great expense to their meager family budget, they were making it possible for me to travel. Then I remember looking out over that park. It was speckled—like a Monet painting—with countless other parents…all lavishing love on *their* children. Right there, my 14-year-old egocentric worldview took a huge hit. I thought, "Wow, those parents love their kids as much as my parents love me. This planet is home to billions of equally lovable children of God." I've carried that understanding with me in my travels ever since.

On the same trip, I sat on the carpet with Norwegian cousins watching the Apollo moon landing. As Neil Armstrong took that first step on the moon, my relatives heard his famous sentence translated into Norwegian:

"*Ett lite skritt for et menneske, ett stort skritt menneskeheten.*" Sharing the excitement of everyone in that room, I realized that while this was an American triumph, it was also a human one—one giant leap for mankind indeed—and the entire planet was celebrating.

As an idealistic young adult, I struggled with what I'd do with my one life. I wanted to work hard at something worthwhile and contribute to society. I wondered if it was really noble to teach wealthy Americans to travel. As a child, my earliest image of "travel" was of rich Americans on fancy white cruise ships in the Caribbean, throwing coins off the deck so they could photograph what they called the "little dark kids" jumping in after them. They'd take these photos home as souvenirs of their relative affluence. That was not the kind of travel I wanted to promote.

Even today, remnants of that notion of travel persist. I believe that for many Americans, traveling still means seeing if you can eat five meals a day and still snorkel when you get into port. When I say that at a cruise convention, people fidget nervously. But I'm not condemning cruise vacations. I'm simply saying I don't consider that activity "travel." It's hedonism. (And I don't say that in a judgmental way, either. I've got no problem with hedonism…after all, I'm a Lutheran.) Rather than accentuate the difference between "us" and "them," I believe travel should bring us together. If I'm evangelical about the value of travel, it's the thoughtful and challenging kind of travel—less caloric perhaps…but certainly much more broadening.

And so, since that first trip back in 1969, I've spent a third of my life overseas, living out of a backpack, talking to people who see things differently than me. It makes me a little bit of an odd duck.

For the last 30 years, I've taught people how to travel. I focus mostly on the logistics: finding the right hotel, avoiding long lines, sampling local delicacies, and catching the train on time. But that's not why we travel.

We travel to have enlightening experiences, to meet inspirational people, to be stimulated, to learn, and to grow.

Travel has taught me the fun in having my cultural furniture rearranged and my ethnocentric self-assuredness walloped. It has humbled me, enriched my life, and tuned me in to a rapidly changing world. And for that, I am thankful. In this book, I'll share what has made my travels most rewarding, and how they have helped shape my worldview and inspired my activism.

As a travel teacher, I've been fortunate to draw from a variety of rich overseas experiences. And, since just after 9/11, I've been giving a lecture I call "Travel as a Political Act." I enjoy flying all over the USA, giving this talk to peacenik environmentalists in Boulder, high-society ladies' clubs in Charlotte, homemakers in Toledo, Members of Congress and their aides on Capitol Hill, and at universities across the country.

With this book, I flesh out the message of that talk and trace the roots of my ideas to the actual personal travel experiences from which they origi-nated. While I draw from trips all over the globe, my professional focus is Europe, so most of my anecdotes are set in Europe. Europe is not that exotic, but it's on par with us in development, confidence, and impact on the developing world. Consequently, Europe provides an instructive parallel-yet-different world from which to view the accomplishments of our society and the challenges we face.

I enjoy bettering myself by observing others. And I appreciate constructive criticism from caring friends. In that same spirit, I enjoy learning about my society by observing other societies and challenging myself (and my neighbors) to be broad-minded when it comes to international issues. Holding our country to a high standard and searching for ways to better live up to its lofty ideals is not "America-bashing." It's good citizenship.

I'm unapologetically proud to be an American. The United States has made me who I am. I spend plenty of time in other countries, but the happiest day of any trip is the day I come home. I'd never live abroad, and I'd certainly not have as much fun running my business overseas as I do here at home. America is a great and innovative nation that the world understandably looks to for leadership. But other nations have some pretty good ideas, too. By learning from our travels and bringing these ideas home, we can make our nation even stronger. As a nation of immigrants whose very origin is based on the power of diversity ("out of many, one"), this should come naturally to us...and be celebrated.

This book isn't a preachy political treatise. (At least, I hope it isn't.) Since I'm a travel writer at heart, this book is heavy on travel tales and people-to-people connections. My premise is that thoughtful travel comes with powerful lessons. With this book, I hope to inspire others to travel more purposefully.

I'll draw conclusions throughout...not always confident that I'm right. My goal is not to be "right" all the time, but to learn with an open mind, to consider new solutions to old problems, to come home and look more honestly into the mirror, and to become involved in helping our society confront its challenges more wisely.

By the nature of this book, you'll get a lot of my opinions. My opinions are shaped by who I am. Along with being a traveler, I'm a historian, Christian, husband, parent, carnivore, musician, capitalist, minimalist, member of NORML, and a workaholic. I've picked up my progressive politics (and my favorite ways to relax) largely from the people I've met overseas. And I seem to end up teaching everything I love: history, music, travel...and now, politics.

Your opinions will differ from mine because we draw from different life experiences. As a writer, I'll try not to abuse my bully pulpit. Still, rather than take the edge off of my opinions, I'll share them with the knowledge that good people will respectfully disagree with each other. I've always marveled at how passionate I am when my Dad and I disagree on some political issue. He's my flesh and blood. Often his political assessment of something will exasperate me. I love him—but how can he possibly believe these things? While I don't necessarily want him to change his mind, I want him to understand my perspective. Sharing it with him consumes me. In writing this book, I've discovered a similar passion. I want to share what I've learned with my fellow Americans...because I consider us all part of one big family. And I assume that you're reading this book for the same reason that I wrote it: because we both care.

In the following chapter, I lay out the framework—the fundamental skills—that have helped me open up my perspective. Then we'll travel together to seven very different destinations. By the time we return home, I hope that—as on any good trip—we'll have a richer understanding of our world.

Chapter 1
How to Travel as a Political Act

If this book is a trip featuring seven exciting destinations, this first chapter is the flight over—a great time to mentally prepare for a trip. To get the most value out of your travels, plan to get out of your comfort zone, meet the people, and view other cultures—as well as our own—with an open mind. Here's how I do it. (I'll try to make it worth missing the in-flight movie.)

Travel like a Medieval Jester

I'm a travel writer. According to conventional wisdom, injecting politics into your travel writing is not good for business. Isn't travel, after all, a form of recreational escapism? Yes...but it can be much more.

For me, since about 9/12, the role of a travel writer has changed. I see the travel writer of the 21st century like the court jester of the Middle Ages. While thought of as a jokester, the jester was in a unique position to tell truth to power without being punished. Back then, kings were absolute rulers—detached from the lives of their subjects. The court jester's job was to mix it up with people that the king would never meet. The jester would play in the gutter with the riffraff. Then, having fingered the gritty pulse of society, he'd come back into the court and tell the king the truth. "Your Highness, the people are angered by the cost of mead. They are offended by the queen's parties. The pope has more influence than you. Everybody is reading the heretics' pamphlets. Your stutter is the butt of many rude jokes." The king didn't kill the jester. In order to rule more wisely, the king needed the jester's insights.

Many of today's elected leaders have no better connection with real people (especially outside their borders) than those "divinely ordained" kings did centuries ago. And while I'm fortunate to have a built-in platform, I believe that any traveler can play jester to their own communities. Whether visiting El Salvador (where people *don't* dream of having two cars in every garage), Denmark (where they pay high taxes with high expectations and are satisfied), or Iran (where many willingly compromised their freedom to be ruled by clerics out of fear that, as they explained to me, their little girls would be raised to be sex toys), any traveler can bring back valuable insights. And, just like those truths were needed in the Middle Ages, this understanding is needed in our age.

Choosing to Travel on Purpose

Ideally, travel broadens our perspectives personally, culturally, and politically. Suddenly, the palette with which we paint the story of our lives has more colors. We realize there are exciting alternatives to the social and community norms that our less-traveled neighbors may never consider. Imagine not knowing you could eat "ethnic." Imagine suddenly realizing there were different genres of music. Imagine you loved books and one day the librarian mentioned there was an upstairs.

Whether you travel as a monk, a hedonist, or somewhere in between, you can come home better friends with our world.

But you can only reap these rewards of travel if you're open to them. Watching a dervish whirl can be a cruise-ship entertainment option...or a spiritual awakening. You can travel to relax and have fun. You can travel to learn and broaden your perspective. Or, best of all, you can do both at once. Make a decision that on any trip you take, you'll make a point to be open to new experiences, seek options that get you out of your comfort zone, and be a cultural chameleon—trying on new ways of looking at things and striving to become a "temporary local."

Assuming they want to learn, both monks and hedonists can stretch their perspectives through travel. While your choice of destination has a huge impact on the potential for learning, you don't need to visit refugee camps to gain political insight. With the right approach, meeting people—whether over beer in an Irish pub, while hiking Himalayan ridges, or sharing fashion tips in Iran—can connect you more thoughtfully with our world.

My best vacations have been both fun and intensely educational. Seeing how smart people overseas come up with fresh new solutions to the same old problems makes me more humble, open to creative solutions, and ready to question traditional ways of thinking. We understand how our worldview is both shaped and limited by our family, friends, media, and

Good people have different passions.

cultural environment. We become more able to respectfully coexist with people with different "norms" and values.

Travel challenges truths that we were raised thinking were self-evident and God-given. Leaving home, we learn other people find different truths to be self-evident. We realize that it just makes sense to give everyone a little wiggle room.

Traveling in Bulgaria, you learn that shaking your head "no" means yes, and giving an affirmative nod can mean no. In restaurants in France, many travelers, initially upset that "you can't even get the bill," learn that slow service is respectful service—you've got the table all night…please take your time. And learning how Atatürk heroically and almost single-handedly pulled Turkey out of the Middle Ages and into the modern world in the 1920s explains why today's Turks are quick to see his features in passing clouds.

Traveling thoughtfully, we are inspired by the accomplishments of other people, communities, and nations. And getting away from our home turf and looking back at America from a distant vantage point, we see ourselves as others see us—an enlightening if not always flattering view.

Connect with People

One of the greatest rewards of travel comes from the people you encounter—especially if you're open to letting them show off a bit and impress you with their culture. As a traveler, I make a point to be a cultural lint brush—trying to pick up whatever cultural insights I can glean from every person I meet.

In our daily routines, we tend to surround ourselves with people more or less like us. It's the natural thing to do. But on the road, you meet people you'd never connect with at home. In my travels, I meet a greater variety of interesting people in two months than I do in an entire year back home. I view each of these chance encounters as loaded with potential to teach me about people and places so different from my hometown world.

For example, one of my favorite countries is Ireland—not because of its sights, but because of its people. Travel in Ireland gives me the sensation that I'm actually understanding a foreign language. And the Irish have that marvelous "gift of gab." They love to talk. For them, conversation is an art form.

Actually, more Irish speak Irish (their native Celtic tongue) than many travelers realize. Very often you'll step into a shop, not realizing the locals there are talking to each other in Irish. They turn to you and switch to English, without missing a beat. When you leave, they slip right back into their Irish.

The best place to experience Ireland is in a Gaeltacht, as Irish-speaking regions are called. These are government-subsidized national preserves for traditional lifestyles. In a Gaeltacht, it seems like charming and talkative locals conspire to slow down anyone with too busy an itinerary.

Ireland gives me the sensation of understanding a foreign language...with people who love to talk.

I was deep into one conversation with an old-timer. We were on the far west coast of the Emerald Isle—where they squint out at the Atlantic and say, "Ahhh, the next parish over is Boston." I asked my new friend, "Were you born here?" He said, "No, 'twas 'bout five miles down the road." Later, I asked him, "Have you lived here all your life?" He winked and said, "Not yet."

In even the farthest reaches of the globe, travelers discover a powerful local pride. Guiding a tour group through eastern Turkey, I once dropped in on a craftsman who was famous for his wood carving. Everybody in that corner of Turkey wanted a prayer niche in their mosque carved by him. We gathered around his well-worn work table. He had likely never actually met an American. And now he had 15 of us gathered around his table. He was working away and showing off…clearly very proud. Then suddenly he stopped, held his chisel high into the sky, and declared, "A man and his chisel—the greatest factory on earth."

Looking at him, it was clear he didn't need me to tell him about fulfillment. When I asked if I could buy a piece of his art, he said, "For a man my age to know that my work will go back to the United States and be appreciated, that's payment enough. Please take this home with you, and remember me."

I traveled through Afghanistan long before the word Taliban entered our lexicon. While there, I enjoyed lessons highlighting the pride and diversity you'll find across the globe. I was sitting in a Kabul cafeteria popular with backpacking travelers. I was just minding my own business when a local man sat next to me. He said, "Can I join you?" I said, "You already have." He said, "You're an American, aren't you?" I said yes, and he said, "Well, I'm a professor here in Afghanistan. I want you to know that a third of the people on this planet eat with their spoons and forks like you, a third of the people eat with chopsticks, and a third of the people eat with fingers like me. And we're all just as civilized."

As he clearly had a chip on his shoulder about this, I simply thought, "Okay, okay, I get it." But I didn't get it…at least, not right away. After leaving Afghanistan, I traveled through South Asia, and his message stayed with me. I went to fancy restaurants filled with well-dressed local professionals. Rather than providing silverware, they had a ceremonial sink in the middle of the room. People would wash their hands and use their fingers for what God made them for. I did the same. Eventually eating with my fingers became quite natural. (I had to be retrained when I got home.)

Stow Your Preconceptions and Be Open to New Experiences

Along with the rest of our baggage, we tend to bring along knee-jerk assumptions about what we expect to encounter abroad. Sometimes these can be helpful (remember to drive on the left in Britain). Other times, they can interfere with our ability to fully engage with the culture on its own terms.

People tell me that they enjoy my public television shows and my guidebooks because I seem like just a normal guy. I'll take that as a compliment. What can I say? I'm simple. I was raised thinking cheese is orange and the shape of the bread. Slap it on and—*voilà!*...cheese sandwich.

But in Europe, I quickly learned that cheese is not orange nor the shape of the bread. In France alone, you could eat a different cheese every day of the year. And it wouldn't surprise me if people did. The French are passionate about their cheese.

I used to be put off by sophisticates in Europe. Those snobs were so enamored with their fine wine and stinky cheese, and even the *terroir* that created it all. But now I see that, rather than showing off, they're simply proud and eager to share. By stowing my preconceptions and opening myself up to new experiences, I've achieved a new appreciation for all sorts of highbrow stuff I thought I'd never really "get." Thankfully, people are sophisticated about different things, and I relish the opportunity to meet and learn from an expert while traveling. I'm the wide-eyed bumpkin...and it's a cultural show-and-tell.

If they're evangelical about cheese, raise your hands and say hallelujah.

For example, I love it when my favorite restaurateur in Paris, Marie-Alice, takes me shopping in the morning and shows me what's going to shape her menu that night. We enter her favorite cheese shop—a fragrant festival of mold. Picking up the moldiest, gooiest wad, Marie-Alice takes a deep whiff, and whispers, "Oh, Rick, smell zees cheese. It smells like zee feet of angels."

Family Pride and Fine Wine

I've been inspired by how the pride of a family business or regional specialty stays strong, generation after generation. In Italy's Umbria region, I have long taken my tour groups to the Bottai family vineyard. Cecilia, the oldest daughter, is no longer the little girl that I once knew. Now, as her parents are taking it easy, she greets us at the gate and shares the family's passion with us. Cecilia walks us through the vineyard, introducing grape plants to us as if they were her children. As we follow her into the dark, cool tunnels of her vast cellar—dug a thousand years ago—she finds just the right bottle to share. And finally, we gather at the family dining table in a room that has changed little in 200 years.

On my last visit, I remember enjoying Cecilia's pride and happiness as she popped open that bottle of their fine Orvieto Classico wine. Watching my glass fill, I noticed her

When your name's on the label, you take great joy in sharing.

hand gripped the bottle in a way that framed the family name on the label. And I noticed how her mother and now-frail grandmother looked on silently and proudly as visitors from the other side of the world gathered in their home. On that remote farm in Italy, where the Bottai family had been producing wine for countless generations, my group was tasting the fruit of their land, labor, and culture. And our hosts were beaming with joy.

Take History Seriously—Don't Be Dumbed Down

Contrary to conventional wisdom, a history degree is practical. Back when I got my degree, I was encouraged to also earn a business degree, so I'd leave the university with something "useful." I believe now that if more Americans had a history degree and put it to good use, this world would be better off. Yesterday's history informs today's news...which becomes tomorrow's history. Those with a knowledge of history can understand current events in a broader context and respond to them more thoughtfully.

As you travel, opportunities to enjoy history are everywhere. Work on cultivating a general grasp of the sweep of history, and you'll be able to infuse your sightseeing with more meaning.

Where can a monkey spy two seas and two continents at the same time? On the Rock of Gibraltar.

I was sitting on the summit of the Rock of Gibraltar, looking out at Africa. It's the only place on earth where you can see two continents and two seas at the same time. The straits were churning with action. Where bodies of water meet, they create riptides— confused, choppy teepee seas that stir up plankton, attracting little fish, birds, bigger fish...and fishermen balancing the risks and rewards of working those churning waters. The fertile straits are also busy with hungry whales, dolphins, and lots of ferries and maritime traffic. Boats cut through feeding grounds, angering environmentalists. And windsurfers catch a stiff breeze, oblivious to it all.

Looking out over the action, with the Pillars of Hercules in the misty Moroccan distance, I realized that there was also a historical element in this combustible mix. Along with seas and continents, this is where, for many centuries, two great civilizations—Islam and Christendom—have come together, creating cultural riptides. Centuries after Muslims from North Africa conquered Catholic Spain, Spain eventually triumphed, but was irrevocably changed in the process. Where civilizations meet, there are risks... and rewards. It can be dangerous, it can be fertile, and it shapes history.

Later that day—still pondering Islam and Christendom rubbing like tectonic plates—I stepped into a small Catholic church. Throughout Spain, churches display statues of a hero called "St. James the Moor-Slayer." And every Sunday, good 21st-century Christians sit—probably listening to sermons about tolerance—under this statue of James, his sword raised, heroic on his rearing horse, with the severed heads of Muslims tumbling all around him. It becomes even more poignant when you realize that the church is built upon the ruins of a mosque, which was built upon the ruins of a church, which was built upon the ruins of a Roman temple, which was built upon the ruin of an earlier pagan holy place. Standing in that church, it occurred to me that the recent friction between Christendom and Islam is nothing new and nothing we can't overcome. But it's more than the simple shoot-'em-up with good guys and bad guys, as often presented to us by politicians and the media. Travel, along with a sense of history, helps us better understand its full complexity.

News in modern times is history in the making, and travelers can actually be eyewitnesses to history as it unfolds. I was in Berlin in 1999, just as their renovated parliament building re-opened to the public. For a generation, this historic Reichstag building—upon whose rooftop some of the last fighting of World War II occurred—was a bombed-out and blackened hulk, overlooking the no-man's-land between East and West Berlin. After unification, Germany's government returned from Bonn to Berlin. And, in good European style, the Germans didn't bulldoze their historic capitol building. Instead, recognizing the building's cultural roots, they renovated it—incorporating modern architectural design, and capping it with a glorious glass dome.

Germany's old-meets-new parliament building comes with powerful architectural symbolism. It's free to enter, open long hours, and designed for German citizens to climb its long spiral ramp to the very top and literally look down (through a glass ceiling) over the shoulders of their legislators to see what's on their desks. The Germans, who feel they've been manipulated by too many self-serving politicians over the last century, are determined to keep a closer eye on their leaders from now on.

Spiraling slowly up the ramp to the top of the dome during that festive

In the 21st century, "St. James the Moor-Slayer" still gets a place of honor in many Spanish churches.

The new glass dome atop Germany's parliament building comes with a point.

opening week, I was surrounded by teary-eyed Germans. Now, anytime you're surrounded by teary-eyed Germans... something exceptional is going on. Most of those teary eyes were old enough to remember the difficult times after World War II, when their city lay in rubble. For these people, the opening of this grand building was the symbolic closing of a difficult chapter in the history of a great nation. No more division. No more fascism. No more communism. They had a united government and were entering a new century with a new capitol filled with hope and optimism.

It was a thrill to be there. I was caught up in it. But then, as I looked around at the other travelers up there with me, I realized that only some of us fully grasped what was going on. Many tourists seemed so preoccupied with trivialities—forgotten camera batteries, needing a Coke, the lack of air-conditioning—that they were missing out on this once-in-a-lifetime opportunity to celebrate a great moment with the German people. And it saddened me. I thought, "I don't want to be part of a dumbed-down society."

I worry that the mainstream tourism industry encourages us to be dumbed down. To many people, travel is only about having fun in the sun, shopping duty-free, and cashing in frequent-flyer miles. But to me, that stuff distracts us from the real thrills, rewards, and value of travel. In our travels—and in our everyday lives—we should become more educated about and engaged with challenging issues, using the past to understand the present. The more you know, and the more you strive to learn, the richer your travels and your life become.

In my own realm as a travel teacher, when I have the opportunity to lead a tour, write a guidebook, or make a TV show, I take it with the responsibility to respect and challenge the intellect of my tour members, readers, or viewers. All of us will gain more from our travels if we refuse to be dumbed down. Promise yourself and challenge your travel partners to be engaged and grapple with the challenging issues while on the road. Your experience will be better for it.

Overcome Fear

Fear has always been a barrier to travel. And, after 9/11, the US became even more fearful...and more isolated. Of course, there are serious risks that deserve our careful attention. But it's all too easy to mistake fear for actual danger. Franklin D. Roosevelt's assertion that we have nothing to fear but fear itself feels just as relevant today as when he first said it in 1933.

I'm hardly a fearless traveler. I can think of many times I've been afraid before a trip. Years ago, I heard that in Egypt, the beggars were relentless, there were no maps, and it was so hot that car tires melted to the streets. For three years, I had plane tickets to India but bailed out, finding other places closer to my comfort zone. Before flying to Iran to film a public television show, I was uneasy. But in each case, when I finally went to these countries, I realized my fears were unfounded.

History is rife with examples of leaders who manipulate fear to distract, mislead, and undermine the will of the very people who entrusted them with power. Our own recent history is no exception. If you want to sell weapons to Colombia, exaggerate the threat of drug lords. If you want to build a wall between the US and Mexico, trump up the fear of illegal immigrants.

If you want to create an expensive missile-defense system, terrify people with predictions of nuclear holocaust. My travels have taught me to have a healthy skepticism toward those who peddle fear. And in so many cases, I've learned that the flipside of fear is understanding.

As travelers and as citizens, we react not to the risk of terrorism but to the perceived risk of terrorism—which we generally seem to exaggerate. For travelers, the actual risk is minuscule. Here are the facts: Year after year, about 12 million Americans go to Europe, and not one is killed by terrorists. In 2004, there was a horrific bombing in Madrid—no Americans killed. In 2005, there was a despicable bombing in London's subway and bus system—no Americans killed. In 2008, there was a terrible bombing in Istanbul—no Americans killed. This isn't a guarantee. Tomorrow an American could be beheaded by a terrorist in Madrid. But, tragic as that might be, it wouldn't change the fact that it is safe to travel.

Statistically, even in the most sobering days of post-9/11 anxiety, travel to most international destinations remained no more dangerous than a drive to your neighborhood grocery store.

Why do we react so strongly to these events? The mainstream media are partly to blame. Sensationalizing tragedy gets more eyes on the screen. But it also exaggerates the impact of a disaster, causing viewers (understandably) to overreact. More than once, I've found myself in a place that was going through a crisis that made international headlines—terrorist bombing, minor earthquake, or riots. Folks from back home call me, their voices shaking with anxiety, to be sure I'm okay. They seem surprised when I casually dismiss their concern. Invariably, the people who live in that place are less worked up than the ones watching it on the news 5,000 miles away. I don't blame my loved ones for worrying. The media has distorted the event in their minds.

I got an email recently from a man who wrote, "Thanks for the TV shows. They will provide a historical documentation of a time when Europe was white and not Muslim. Keep filming your beloved Europe before it's gone."

Reading this, I thought how feisty fear has become in our society. A fear of African Americans swept the USA in the 1960s. Jews have been feared in many places throughout history. And today, Muslims are feared. But we have a choice whether or not to be afraid. Americans who have had the opportunity to travel in moderate Muslim nations like Turkey or Morocco—and been welcomed by smiling locals who gush, "We love Americans!"—no longer associate Islam with terrorism.

Of course, terrorism—which, by its very nature, is designed to be emotional and frighten the masses—makes it more difficult to overcome fear. But my travels have helped me distinguish between the fear of terrorism… and the actual danger of terrorism. I was in London on 7/7/05, a date the Brits consider "their 9/11." A series of devastating bombs ripped through the subway system, killing 52 and injuring about 700 people. Remembering the impact of 9/11 on the United States, I thought, "Oh my goodness, everything will be shut down."

Instead, I witnessed a country that, as a matter of principle, refused to be terrorized by the terrorists. The prime minister returned from meetings in Scotland to organize a smart response. Within a couple of days, he was back in Scotland, London was functioning as normal, and they set out to catch the bad guys—which they did. There was no lingering panic. People mourned the tragedy, even as they kept it in perspective. The terrorists were

Reducing the tragedy of terrorist casualties to statistics strikes many people as disrespectful and callous. But I believe that when we overreact to the threat of the terrorist, we empower the terrorist and actually become part of the problem. By setting emotion aside and being as logical as possible, we can weigh the relative risks and rewards or costs and benefits of various American behaviors.

Every three days, a 747's worth of people die on our highways. And it's not worth headlines. We're a mighty nation of 300 million people. People die. Some 40,000 people die on our roads every year. Anybody in that business knows if we all drove 20 miles an hour slower, we'd save thousands of precious lives. But in the privacy of the voting booth, is the average American going to vote to drive 50 mph on our freeways to save thousands of lives? Hell, no. We've got places to go.

Consider handguns. Thirteen thousand people die every year in our country because of handguns. You could make the case that that's a reasonable price to pay for the precious right to bear arms. We are a free and well-educated democracy. We know the score. And year after year, we seem to agree that spending these lives is a reasonable trade-off for enjoying our Second Amendment right.

Germans decided not to have that right to bear arms, and consequently they lose only about 1,000 people a year. Europeans (who suffer less than a quarter the per capita gun killings we

do) laugh out loud when they hear that Americans are staying home for safety reasons. If you care about your loved ones (and understand the statistics), you'll take them to Europe tomorrow.

If we dispassionately surveyed the situation, we might similarly accept the human cost of our aggressive stance on this planet. We spend untold thousands of lives a year for the rights to drive fast and bear arms. Perhaps 300 million Americans being seen by the rest of the world as an empire is another stance that comes with an unavoidable cost in human lives.

I know this is wild, but imagine we downgraded our "War on Terror." Fantasize for a moment about the money and energy we could save, and all the good we could do with those resources if they were compassionately and wisely diverted to challenges like global warming or the plight of desperate people (in lands that have no oil or strategic importance) whose suffering barely registers in the media. Imagine then the resulting American image abroad. We'd be tougher for our terrorist enemies to demonize. And imagine the challenge that would present to terrorist recruiters.

captured and brought to justice, Britain made a point to learn from the event (by reviewing security on public transit and making an effort to interact more constructively with its Muslim minority)...and life went on.

The American reaction to the shocking and grotesque events of 9/11 was understandable. But seeing another society respond so differently to its own disaster inspired me to grapple with a new perspective. If the goal of terrorists is to terrify us into submission, then those who refuse to become fearful stand defiantly against them.

Every time I'm stuck in a long security line at the airport, I reflect on one of the most disconcerting results of terrorism: The very people who would benefit most from international travel—those who needlessly fear people and places they don't understand—decide to stay home. I believe the most powerful things an individual American can do to fight terrorism are to travel a lot, learn about the world, come home with a new perspective, and then work to help our country fit more comfortably and less fearfully into this planet.

The American Dream, Bulgarian Dream, Sri Lankan Dream: Celebrate Them All

I fondly remember the confusion I felt when I first met someone who wouldn't trade passports with me. I thought, "I've got more wealth, more freedom, more opportunity than you'll ever have—why wouldn't you want what I've got?" I assumed anyone with half a brain would aspire to the American Dream. But the vast majority of non-Americans don't. They have the Bulgarian Dream, or the Sri Lankan Dream, or the Moroccan Dream. Thanks to travel, this no longer surprises me. In fact, I celebrate it.

I was raised thinking the world is a pyramid with us on top and everybody else trying to get there. Well into my adulthood, I actually believed that if another country didn't understand that they should want to be like us, we had every right to go in and elect a government for them that did.

While I once unknowingly cheered on cultural imperialism, travel has taught me that one of the ugliest things one nation can do is write another nation's textbooks. Back in the Cold War, I had a Bulgarian friend who attended an English-language high school in Sofia. I read his Soviet-produced textbooks, which were more concerned about ideology than teaching. He learned about "economics" with no mention of Adam Smith. And I've seen what happens when the US funds the publishing of textbooks in places such as El Salvador and Nicaragua, with ideological strings attached. The economics of a banana republic are taught in a way that glorifies multinational corporation tactics and vilifies heroes of popular indigenous movements. I think most Americans would be appalled if we knew how many textbooks we're writing in the developing world.

On the road, you learn that ethnic underdogs everywhere are waging valiant but seemingly hopeless struggles. When assessing

This family has the Sri Lankan Dream.

their tactics, I remind myself that every year on this planet a dozen or so languages go extinct. That means that many heroic, irreplaceable little nations finally lose their struggle and die. There are no headlines—they just get weaker and weaker until that last person who speaks that language dies... and so does one little bit of ethnic diversity on our planet.

I was raised so proud of Nathan Hale and Patrick Henry and Ethan Allen—patriotic heroes of America's Revolutionary War who wished they had more than one life to give for their country. Having traveled, I've learned that Hales, Henrys, and Allens are a dime a dozen on this planet—each country has their own version.

I believe the US tends to underestimate the spine of other nations. It's comforting to think we can simply "shock-and-awe" our enemies into compliance. This is not only untrue...it's dangerous. Sure, we have the mightiest military in the world. But we don't have a monopoly on bravery or grit. In fact, in some ways, we might be less feisty than hardscrabble, emerging nations that feel they have to scratch and claw for their very survival.

We're comfortable, secure, beyond our revolutionary stage...and well into our Redcoat stage. Regardless of our strength and our righteousness, as long as we have a foreign policy stance that requires a military presence in 130 countries, we will be confronting determined adversaries. We must choose our battles carefully. Travel can help us understand that our potential enemies are not cut-and-run mercenaries, but people with spine motivated by passions and beliefs we didn't even know existed, much less understand.

Growing up in the US, I was told over and over how smart, generous, and free we were. Travel has taught me that the vast majority of humanity is raised with a different view of America. Travelers have a priceless opportunity to see our country through the eyes of other people. I still have the American Dream. But I also respect and celebrate other dreams.

Travel where few Americans venture...and locals find you exotic, too.

Gimme that Old-Time Religion...with an International Spin

The United States may be a Christian nation, but we're certainly not *the* Christian nation. Nor do our Christian values set the worldwide standard for Christian values. As a Lutheran, I was surprised to learn that there are more Lutherans in Namibia than in the US. Even though they wouldn't know what to do with the standard American "green hymnal" and don't bring Jell-O molds to their church picnics, they are as Lutheran as I am. They practice the same faith through a different cultural lens.

While European Christians have similar beliefs to ours, travel in the developing world opens your eyes to new ways of interpreting the Bible. An American or European Christian might define Christ's "preferential option for the poor" or the notion of "sanctity of life" differently from someone who has to put their children to bed hungry every night. While a US Christian may be more concerned about abortion than economic injustice, a Namibian Christian would likely flip-flop those priorities. As for the Biblical Jubilee Year concept (where God—in the Book of Leviticus—calls for the forgiveness of debts and the redistribution of land every fifty years), what rich Christian takes it seriously?

Travel beyond the Christian world offers us invaluable opportunities to be exposed to other, sometimes uncomfortable, perspectives. As an American who understands that we have a solemn commitment to protect

Israel's security, I am unlikely to be able to sympathize with the Palestinian perspective...unless I see the issue from outside my home culture. In Iran recently, I watched an Al-Jazeera report on the American-funded wall being built by Israel around a Palestinian community. Politically, I may understand the rationale and need for this wall. But even without understanding the words of that TV documentary, I could also empathize with the visceral anger Muslims might feel—observing as, brick by brick, their humiliated fellow Muslims had their sunlight literally walled out.

I come away from experiences like this one, not suddenly convinced of an opposing viewpoint...but with a creeping discomfort about my confidence in the way I've always viewed the world. Whether reading the Bible through the eyes of Christians from other cultures, or having your hometown blinders wedged open by looking at another religion a new way, travel can be a powerfully spiritual experience.

Get Beyond Your Comfort Zone—Choose to Be Challenged

I've long been enthusiastic about how travel can broaden your perspective. But I didn't always preach this gospel very smartly. Back in the 1970s, in my early days as a tour organizer and guide, I drove 50 or so people each year around Europe in little minibus tours. I had a passion for getting my travelers beyond their comfort zones. Looking back, I cringe at the crudeness, or even cruelty, of my techniques.

As a 25-year-old hippie-backpacker-turned-tour-organizer, I had a notion that soft and spoiled American travelers would benefit from a little hardship. I'd run tours with no hotel reservations and observe the irony of my tour members (who I cynically suspected were unconcerned about homelessness issues in their own communities) being nervous at the prospect of a night without a bed. If, by mid-afternoon, I hadn't arranged for a hotel, they couldn't focus on my guided town walks. In a wrong-headed attempt to force empathy on my flock, I made a point to let them feel the anxiety of the real possibility of no roof over their heads.

Back when I was almost always younger than anyone on my tour, I made my groups sleep in Munich's huge hippie circus tent. With simple mattresses on a wooden floor and 400 roommates, it was like a cross between Woodstock and a slumber party. One night I was stirred out of my sleep by a woman sitting up and sobbing. With the sound of backpackers rutting in the distance, she whispered, apologetically, "Rick, I'm not taking this so very well."

This memorial in El Salvador remembers loved ones lost fighting the United States.

Of course, I eventually learned that you can't just force people into a rough situation and expect it to be constructive. Today, I am still driven to get people out of their comfort zones and into the real world. But I've learned to do it more gently and in a way that keeps our travelers coming back for more.

For me, seeing towering stacks of wood in Belfast destined to be anti-Catholic bonfires and talking with locals about sectarian hatred helps make a trip to Ireland more than just Guinness and traditional music sessions in pubs. Taking groups to Turkey during the Iraq wars has helped me share a Muslim perspective on that conflict. And I consider visiting a concentration camp memorial a required element of any trip we lead through Germany.

As a tour guide, I make a point to follow up these harsh and perplexing experiences with a "reflections time" where I only facilitate the discussion and let tour members share and sort out their feelings and observations. I've learned that, even with the comfortable refuge of a good hotel, you can choose to travel to complicated places and have a valuable learning experience.

A few years ago, I had an opportunity to hang out on the beach for a vacation in the ritzy Mexican resort of Mazatlán. The enticing beach break coincided with an invitation to go to San Salvador (the capital of El Salvador) to remember Archbishop Oscar Romero on the 25th anniversary of his assassination.

For my vacation, I opted for El Salvador—to share a muggy dorm room, eat rice and beans, be covered in bug bites, and march with people in honor of their martyred hero who stood up to what they consider American imperialism. The march passed a long, shiny, black monument that looks just like our Vietnam memorial. It was busy with mourners and etched with countless names—each a casualty of a civil war their loved ones believed was fought against American interests and American-funded troops. It's not a matter of whether America is good or bad in a certain instance. The fact is, the popular patriotic sentiment "my country, right or wrong"—while embraced by many Americans—is by no means unique to our country. There are good people waging heroic struggles all over the world…some of them against our country.

If you've got a week to spend in Latin America, you can lie on a beach in Mazatlán, you can commune with nature in Costa Rica, or you can grapple with our nation's complex role in a country like El Salvador. I've done all three, and enjoyed each type of trip. But El Salvador was far more memorable than the others. The tourism industry has its own priorities. But as a traveler, you always have the option to choose challenging and educational destinations.

See the Rich/Poor Gap for Yourself

After traveling the world, you come home recognizing that Americans are good people with big hearts. We are compassionate and kind, and operate with the best of intentions. But as citizens of a giant, powerful nation—isolated from the rest of the world by geography, as much as by our wealth—it can be challenging for many Americans to understand that poverty across the sea is as real as poverty across the street. We struggle to grasp the huge gap between the wealthy and the poor. While it may be human nature to choose ignorance when it comes to this reality, it's better character to reckon with it honestly.

Anyone can learn that half of the people on this planet are trying to live on $2 a day, and a billion people are trying to live on $1 a day. You can read that the average lot in life for women on this planet is to spend a good part of their waking hours every day walking for water and firewood. But when you travel to the developing world, you meet those "statistics" face-to-face… and the problem becomes more real.

In San Salvador, I met Beatriz, a mother who lives in a cinderblock house with a corrugated tin roof. From the scavenged two-by-four that holds up her roof, a single wire arcs up to a power line that she tapped into to steal electricity for the bare bulb that lights her world each night. She lives in a ravine the city considers "unfit for habitation." She's there not by choice, but because it's near her work and she can't afford bus fare to live beyond walking distance to the place that pays $6 a day for her labor. Apart from her time at work, she spends half the remaining hours of her day walking for water. Her husband is gone, and she's raising a child. Beatriz is not unusual on this planet. In fact, among women, she's closer to the global norm than most women in the United States.

Imagine the power of a well which, with each pump and gush of water, makes an otherwise thirsty villager think, "Thank you, America."

I went home from that trip and spent $5,000 to pay for my daughter Jackie's braces. I had money left over for whitener. I noticed every kid in Jackie's class has a family that can afford $5,000 for braces. This is not a guilt trip. I work hard and am part of a winning economic system in a stable land that makes this possible. I love my daughter and am proud to give her straight and white teeth.

But I have an appetite to understand Beatriz's world and the reality of structural poverty. I know that for the price of two sets of braces ($10,000), a well could be dug so that a thirsty village of women like Beatriz would not have to walk for water. They would have far more time to spend with their children. I advocate within my world on Beatriz's behalf, and enthusiastically support relief work in the developing world. This is not because I am a particularly good person…but because I have met Beatriz.

Traveling in places like El Salvador enables you to appreciate the gap between rich and poor. And having met those people makes it all the more gratifying to help out as you can.

Okay, Let's Travel…

Now it's time for us to pack up these concepts and hit the road. Through the rest of this book, I'll share seven specific examples of "Travel as a Political Act":

In the former Yugoslavia—Croatia, Bosnia-Herzegovina, and Montenegro—we'll wander through the psychological and physical wreckage left in the aftermath of a tragic war...and ponder the sobering lessons.

Considering the European Union, we'll see how a great society (living in a parallel world to ours) is evolving. The EU is melding together a vast free-trade zone while trying to keep alive the cultural equivalent of the family farm: its ethnic diversity.

Traveling to El Salvador, we'll learn about the impact of globalization and the reality of a poor country at the mercy of a rich country—from its own perspective rather than ours.

In Denmark, by delving into contemporary socialism and a hippie attempt at creating a utopia in a society routinely rated the most content in the world, we'll have a stimulating chance to consider a different formula for societal success.

We'll witness the moderate side of Islam in quickly developing nations by visiting Turkey and Morocco. This helps balance our perspective at a time when the news of Islam is dominated by coverage of extremists and terrorists.

In the Netherlands and Switzerland, we'll compare European and American drug policies, contrasting how two equally affluent and advanced societies deal with the same persistent problem in fundamentally different ways.

Exploring Iran, we'll see how fear and fundamentalism can lead a mighty nation to trade democracy for theocracy, and what happens when the "Axis of Evil" meets the "Great Satan"—from an Iranian perspective.

You can travel with your window rolled up...or your window rolled down.

Finally, I'll explain why flying home from each trip reminds me how thankful I am to live in America, why I believe the rich blessings we enjoy as Americans come with certain stewardship responsibilities, and how we can enrich our lives by employing our new perspective more constructively back home.

Chapter 2
Lessons from the Former Yugoslavia: After the War

Since World War II, Europe has enjoyed unprecedented peace... except in its southeastern Balkan Peninsula. As Yugoslavia broke apart violently in the early 1990s, the rest of the world watched in disbelief, then in horror, as former compatriots tore apart their homeland and each other.

Today—less than two decades later—some parts of the former Yugoslavia are re-emerging as major tourist attractions. In recent years, I've enjoyed trips to countries that once belonged to Yugoslavia, including Croatia, Bosnia-Herzegovina, and Montenegro. As destinations, they offer profound natural beauty, a relaxing ambience, and a warm welcome. Life goes on here. Local people, while not in denial about the war, would rather not be constantly reminded of it. Many think about this ugliness in their past only when tourists ask them about it.

And yet—although I realize that, in some ways, it does a disservice to these places to view them through the lens of war—I can't help but think about those recent horrors as I travel here. Seeing the bruised remnants of Yugoslavia is painful yet wonderfully thought-provoking. And, because this book is about how travel can change the way you think about the world, I hope you (and my Balkan friends) will excuse my narrow focus in this chapter.

We begin at the region's top tourist hotspot—the town of Dubrovnik, in Croatia. Nowhere else in Europe can you go so quickly from easy tourism to lands where today's struggles are so vivid and eye-opening. Within a few hours' drive of Dubrovnik are several new incarnations of old nations, providing rich opportunities to study the roots and the consequences of sectarian struggles.

Red Roofs and Mortar Shells in Dubrovnik

I was ready for a little culture shock. Flying from France to Dubrovnik, I got it. I passed through the mammoth, floodlit walls of Dubrovnik's Old Town and hiked up a steep, tourist-free back lane to my boutique pension perched at the top of Europe's finest fortified port city. Upon reaching my favorite Dubrovnik B&B—a bombed-out ruin until a few years ago—I was greeted by Pero Carević.

Pero uncorked a bottle of *orahovica* (the local grappa-like firewater) and told me his story. He got a monthly retirement check for being wounded in

Showing me the mortar that destroyed his home, Pero smiled.

the war, but was bored and didn't want to live on the tiny government stipend—so he went to work and turned the remains of his Old Town home into a fine guest house.

Hoping to write that evening with a clear head, I tried to refuse Pero's drink. But this is a Slavic land. Remembering times when I was force-fed vodka in Russia by new friends, I knew it was hopeless. Pero made this hooch himself, with green walnuts. As he slugged down a shot, he handed me a glass, wheezing, "Walnut grappa—it recovers your energy."

Pero, whose war injury will be with him for the rest of his life, held up the mangled tail of a mortar shell he pulled out from under his kitchen counter and described how the gorgeous stone and knotty-wood building he grew up in suffered a direct hit in the 1991 siege of Dubrovnik. He put the mortar in my hands. Just as I don't enjoy holding a gun, I didn't enjoy touching the twisted remains of that mortar.

I took Pero's photograph. He held the mortar...and smiled. I didn't want him to hold the mortar and smile...but that's what he did. He seemed determined to smile—as if it signified a personal victory over the destruction the mortar had wrought. It's impressive how people can weather tragedy, rebuild, and move on. In spite of the terrors of war just a couple of decades ago, life here was once again very good and, according to Pero's smile, filled with promise.

From Pero's perch, high above Dubrovnik's rooftops, I studied the countless buildings lassoed within its stout walls. The city is a patchwork of old-fashioned red-tiled roofs. Pero explained that the random arrangement of bright- and dark-toned roof tiles indicates the damage caused by the mortars that were lobbed over the hill by the Serb-dominated Yugoslav National Army in 1991. The new, brighter-colored tiles marked houses that were hit and had been rebuilt. At a glance, it's clear that more than two-thirds of the Old Town's buildings were bombed.

But today, relations between the Croats and their Serb neighbors are on the mend. The bus connecting Dubrovnik to Serb-friendly Montenegro—which was stubbornly discontinued for a decade—is, once again, up and running. And Pero says that, with age, someday all the tiles will fade to exactly the same hue.

Poignant as a visit to Dubrovnik may be, rich rewards await those who push on into the interior of the former Yugoslavia. Dubrovnik—the most touristy and comfortable resort on Croatia's Dalmatian Coast—is an ideal springboard for more scintillating sightseeing...including some sobering lessons in sectarian strife.

The Balkans

We hear the term "the Balkans" now and then, and even if we don't know exactly where that is...we know it's a challenging place. The Balkan Peninsula—a wide swath of land in southeastern Europe, stretching from Hungary to Greece—has long been a crossroads of cultures. Over the centuries, an endless string of

In Dubrovnik, brighter tiles mark homes rebuilt after the shelling.

emperors, crusaders, bishops, and sultans have shaped a region that's extremely diverse...and unusually troubled. These troubles are most profound in the former Yugoslavia—roughly the western half of this peninsula.

Yugoslavia's delicate ethnic balance is notoriously difficult to grasp. The major "ethnicities" of Yugoslavia were all South Slavs—they're descended from the same ancestors and speak closely related languages. The only big difference: They practice different religions. Catholic South Slavs are called Croats; Orthodox South Slavs are called Serbs; and Muslim South Slavs (whose ancestors converted to Islam under Ottoman rule) are called Bosniaks. For the most part, there's no way that a casual visitor can determine the religion or loyalties of the people just by looking at them.

While relatively few people are actively religious here (thanks to the stifling atheism of the communist years), they fiercely identify with their

ethnicity. And, because ethnicity and faith are synonymous, it's easy to mistake the recent conflicts for "religious wars." But in reality, they were about the politics of ethnicity (just as the "Troubles" in Ireland are more about British versus Irish rule than simply a holy war between Catholics and Protestants).

"Yugoslavia" was an artificial union of the various South Slav ethnicities that lasted from the end of World War I until 1991. Following the death of its strong-arm leader Tito, a storm of ethnic divisions, a heritage of fear and mistrust, and a spate of land-hungry politicians plunged Yugoslavia into war. Many consider the conflict a "civil war," and others see it as a series of "wars of independence." However you define the wars, they—and the ethnic cleansing, systematic rape, and other atrocities that accompanied them—were simply horrific. It's almost miraculous that after a few bloody years (1991–1995), the many factions laid down their arms and agreed to peace accords. An uneasy peace—firmer and more inspiring with each passing year—has settled over the region.

And yet, hard feelings linger. As a travel writer, I've seen again and again that talking about this region is fraught with controversy. Every time

I publish an article on the former Yugoslavia, I receive an angry avalanche of mail complaining that I'm "taking sides." (Strangely, I typically hear this complaint from each "side" in equal numbers...which suggests I'm actually succeeding at being impartial.) I believe you could line up a panel of experts from this region—historians from prestigious universities, respected journalists, beloved diplomats—and ask them for their take on a particular issue or historical event...and each one would have a completely different interpretation, presented as fact. One person's war hero is another person's war criminal. One person's freedom fighter is another person's rapist. One person's George Washington is another person's Adolf Hitler. It's aggravating, and yet so human. As an outside observer, the best I can do is to sort through the opinions, force myself to see all sides of the story, collect a few random observations to share as food for thought...and encourage readers to learn from the region's tumult.

But there's no substitute for traveling here in person. Walking with the victims of a war through the ruins of their cities gives you "war coverage" you'd never get in front of a TV. Seeing how former enemies find ways to overcome their animosity and heal; enjoying the new energy that teenagers—whose parents did the fighting—bring to the streets; and observing combatants who followed no rules now raising children in the ruins resulting from their mistakes...leaves a strong impression on any visitor.

Buffalo-Nickel Charm on a Road that Does Not Exist

Looking for a change of pace from Croatia's Dalmatian Coast, I drove from Dubrovnik to the city of Mostar, in Bosnia-Herzegovina. Almost everyone doing this trip takes the scenic coastal route. But I took the back road instead: inland first, then looping north through the Serb part of Bosnia-Herzegovina.

While Bosnia-Herzegovina is one country, the peace accords to end the war here in 1995 gerrymandered it to grant a degree of autonomy to the area where Orthodox Serbs predominate. This Republika Srpska, or "Serbian Republic"—while technically part of Bosnia-Herzegovina—rings the Muslim- and Croat-dominated core of the country on three sides.

When asked for driving tips, Croatians—who, because of ongoing tensions, avoid Republika Srpska—actually insisted that the road I hoped to take didn't even exist. As I drove inland from Dubrovnik, directional signs sent me to the tiny Croatian border town...but ignored the major Serb city of

Trebinje just beyond. Despite warnings from Croats in Dubrovnik, I found plenty past that lonely border.

As I entered bustling and prosperous Trebinje, police with ping-pong paddle stop signs pulled me over to tell me drivers need to have their headlights on at all hours. The "dumb tourist" routine got me off the hook. I withdrew cash at an ATM. Bosnia-Herzegovina's currency is called the "convertible mark." The name goes back to the 1980s, when, like other countries with fractured economies, they tied their currency to a strong one. It was named

In spite of what some said, Bosnia-Herzegovina's Trebinje not only exists, it thrives.

after the German mark and given the same value. Today, while Germany has switched over to the euro, the original German mark lives on (with its original exchange rate) in a quirky way in Bosnia. I stowed a few Bosnian coins as souvenirs. They have the charm of Indian pennies and buffalo nickels.

Coming upon a vibrant market, I had to explore. The produce seemed entirely local. Honey maids eagerly offered me tastes—as if each believed her honey was the sweetest. Small-time farmers—salt-of-the-earth couples as rustic as the dirty potatoes they pulled out of the ground that morning—lovingly displayed their produce on rickety card tables. A tourist here was so rare that there was nothing designed for me to buy. Coming from Croatia, I was primed to think of Serbs as the villains. Wandering through the market, I saw only a hardworking community of farmers offering a foreigner a warm if curious welcome.

As I left Trebinje and continued on the road, it became apparent that the complex nature of things here comes across in the powerful language of flags. Just as bars throughout Europe don't want football team colors, and pubs throughout Ireland don't want the green or orange of the sectarian groups, flags in this region come with lots of pent-up political anger. Throughout the day I saw different flags, each one flying with an agenda. Croats salute their red-and-white checkerboard flag, while Serbs proudly hoist their flag with four C's (the first letter of "Serb" in the Cyrillic alphabet). But in the not-too-distant past, each of these flags was also employed by an oppressive regime—so Croats and Serbs each view the other's flag as equivalent to a swastika. Meanwhile, the country's official flag—which nobody really embraces (or is offended by)—is a yellow-and-blue, triangle-and-stars configuration dreamed up by the European Union.

While most tourists can't tell the difference, locals notice subtle clues that indicate they're entering a different ethnicity's home turf—those highly symbolic flags, discreet but hateful graffiti symbols, new road signs with politically charged names, and even ATMs with instructions in Croatian, Bosnian, or Serbian—but not the other two languages. During the days of Yugoslavia, these languages were all lumped together into a single, mutually intelligible mother tongue called "Serbo-Croatian." But, stoked by the patriotism of proud new nationhood, each of these groups has artificially distanced its language from the others—inventing new words to replace ones they find "too Serbian" or "too Croatian."

Later, after a two-hour drive on deserted roads through a rugged landscape, I arrived at the humble Serb crossroads village of Nevesinje. Towns in this region all have a "café row," and Nevesinje is no exception. It was lunchtime, but as I walked through the town, I didn't see a soul with any food on the table—just drinks. In this village, where unemployment is epidemic, apparently locals eat cheaply at home...and then enjoy an affordable coffee or drink at a café.

A cluttered little grocery—with a woman behind the counter happy to make a sandwich—was my answer for lunch. The salami looked like Spam. Going through the sanitary motions, she laid down a piece of waxed paper to catch the meat—but the slices landed wetly on the grotty base of the slicer as they were cut. A strong cup of "Bosnian coffee" (we'd call it "Turkish coffee")—with highly caffeinated, loose grounds settled in the bottom—cost just pennies in the adjacent café. Munching my sandwich and sipping the coffee carefully to avoid the mud, I watched the street scene.

Nevesinje teens gather to see class photos.

Big men drove by in little beaters. High-school students crowded around the window of the local photography shop, which had just posted their class graduation photos. The schoolgirls on this cruising drag proved you don't need money to have style. Through a shop window, I could see a newly engaged couple picking out a ring. One moment I saw Nevesinje as very different from my hometown...and the next it seemed essentially the same.

And then, as my eyes wandered to the curiously overgrown ruined building across the street, I noticed bricked-up, pointed Islamic arches...and realized it was once a mosque. As if surveying a horrible crime scene, I had to walk through its backyard. It was a no-man's land of broken concrete and glass. A single half-knocked-over, turban-shaped tombstone still managed to stand. The prayer niche inside, where no one prays anymore, faced a vacant lot.

The idea that there had recently been a bloody war in this country is abstract until you actually come here. Walking these streets, I talked with locals about the cruel quirkiness of this war. The towns that got off relatively easy were the ones with huge majorities of one or the other faction. Towns with the most bloodshed and destruction were the most diverse—where no single ethnic group dominated. Because Nevesinje was a predominantly Orthodox town, the Serbs killed or forced out the Muslims and destroyed their mosque. Surviving Muslim refugees reportedly had to walk for a week over a mountain pass to safety in Mostar—where, Serbs like to say, "They found better living conditions anyway."

Remaining impartial is an ongoing challenge. It's so tempting to think of the Muslims—who were brutalized in many parts of Bosnia-Herzegovina—as the "victims." But when traveling here, I have to keep reminding myself that elsewhere in this conflict, Serbs or Croats were victimized in much the same way. Early in the war, outcast Serbs migrated to safety in the opposite direction—from Mostar to Nevesinje. On the hillside overlooking

Mostar are the ruins of a once-magnificent Serbian Orthodox church—now demolished, just like that mosque in Nevesinje. Travel allows you to fill out a balanced view of a troubled region.

Considering the haphazardness of war, I remembered how in France's charming Alsace (the region bordering Germany), all towns go back centuries—but those with the misfortune to be caught in the steamroller of war don't have a building standing from before 1945. I recalled that in England, Chester survived while nearby Coventry was leveled so thoroughly that the Germans had a new word for bombing to smithereens—to "coventrate" a place. And I remembered the confused patchwork of Dubrovnik's old and new tile roofs. These images—and now this sad, ruined mosque—all humanized the bleak reality and random heartbreak of sectarian strife and war.

Ready to move on, I climbed into my little car, left Nevesinje, and drove out of the mountains. My destination was a city that once symbolized East and West coming together peacefully, then symbolized just the opposite, and today seems to be enjoying a tentative new spirit of peaceful coexistence: Mostar.

A ruined mosque is a silent reminder of sectarian fighting in a now thoroughly Serbian, and therefore Orthodox Christian, town.

Bosnian Hormones and a Shiny New Cemetery

Exploring the city of Mostar—with its vibrant humanity and the persistent reminders of its recent and terrible war—was both exhilarating and exhausting.

Mostar represents the best and the worst of Yugoslavia. During the Tito years, it was an idyllic mingling of cultures—Catholic Croats, Orthodox Serbs, and Muslim Bosniaks living together in relative harmony, their differences spanned by an Old Bridge that symbolized an optimistic vision of a Yugoslavia where ethnicity didn't matter. And yet, as the country unraveled in the early 1990s, Mostar was gripped by a gory three-way war among those same groups. Not that long ago, the people I now encountered here—those who set me up at a computer terminal in the cybercafé, stopped for me when I jaywalked, showed off their paintings, and directed the church choir—had been killing each other.

Mostar's 400-year-old, Turkish-style stone bridge—with its elegant, single, pointed arch—was symbolic of the town's status as the place where East met West in Europe. Then, during the 1990s, Mostar became the

Mostar's beloved, Turkish-style Old Bridge is rebuilt and once again brings hope that East and West can meet and mix gracefully.

tragic poster child of the Bosnian war. Across the world, people felt the town's pain when its beloved bridge—bombarded for days from the hilltop above—finally collapsed into the river.

Now the bridge has been rebuilt, and Mostar is putting itself back together. But the scars of war are still evident. The Serbs who once lived here have fled deeper into the countryside, into the Republika Srpska. The two groups who still live here are effectively segregated along the front line that divided them during wartime: the Muslims on the east side and the Croats on the west. While the two groups are making some efforts at reintegration, progress is slow. In 2005, some young Mostarians unveiled a statue of Bruce Lee, who they saw as symbolizing the fight for positive values that all sides could identify with. Lee, who struggled against ethnic divisions between Chinese and Americans, represented to the people of Mostar an inspirational bridging of cultures. Sadly, two days after the unveiling, the statue was vandalized.

But there is progress. As I explored the workaday streets of the town, it seemed that—despite the war damage—Mostar was downright thriving. Masala Square (literally "Place for Prayer" square) is designed for big gatherings. Muslim groups meet at the square before departing for Mecca on their pilgrimage, or Hajj. But on the night of my visit, there was not a hint of prayer. It was prom night. The kids were out...Bosnian hormones were raging. Being young and sexy is a great equalizer. With a beer, loud music, desirability, twinkling stars...and no war...your family's income and your country's GDP hardly matter. Today's 18-year-old Mostarian was a toddler during the war. Looking at these kids and their dried-apple grandparents clad in dusty black, warming benches on the "Place for Prayer" square, I imagined that there must be quite a generation gap.

I was swirling in a snow globe of teenagers, and through the commotion, a thirtysomething local came at me with a huge smile: Alen from Orlando. Actually, he's from Mostar, but fled to Florida during the war and now spends summers with his family here. A fan of my public television series, he immediately offered to show me around his hometown.

Alen's local perspective gave Mostar meaning. He pointed to a fig tree growing out of a small minaret. Seeming to speak as much about Mostar's people as its vegetation, Alen said, "It's a strange thing in nature...figs can grow with almost no soil." There were blackened ruins from the war everywhere. When I asked why—after nearly two decades—the ruins had not been touched, Alen explained, "There's confusion about who owns what.

Surviving companies have no money. The Bank of Yugoslavia, which held the mortgages, is now gone. No one will invest until it's clear who owns the buildings." I had never considered the financial confusion that follows the breakup of a country, and how it could stunt a society's redevelopment.

We walked to a small cemetery congested with more than a hundred white-marble Muslim tombstones. Alen pointed out the dates: Everyone died in 1993, 1994, or 1995. Before 1993, this was a park. When the war heated up, snipers were a constant concern—they'd pick off anyone they saw walking down the street. Because of the ongoing danger, bodies were left for weeks, rotting on the main boulevard, which had become the front line. Mostar's cemeteries were too exposed to be used, but this tree-filled park was relatively safe from snipers. People buried their neighbors here...under the cover of darkness.

Weaving slowly through the tombstones, Alen explained, "In those years, night was the time when we lived. We didn't walk...we ran. And we dressed in black. There was no electricity. If the Croats didn't kill us with their bullets, they killed us with their music." That politically charged, rabble-rousing Croatian pop music, used—apparently effectively—as a kind of psychological torture, was blasting constantly from the Croat side of town.

On Mostar's main square, children of former combatants embrace life...and are ready to party.

This cemetery, once a park, is filled with tombstones all dated 1993, 1994, or 1995.

As we wandered through town, the sectarian symbolism of the conflict was powerful. Ten minarets pierced Mostar's skyline like proud Muslim exclamation points. Across the river, twice as high as the tallest minaret, stood the Croats' new Catholic church spire. Standing on the reconstructed Old Bridge, I looked at the hilltop high above the town, with its single, bold, and strongly floodlit cross. Alen said, "We Muslims believe that cross marks the spot from where they shelled this bridge. They built it there, and floodlight it each night...like a celebration."

The next day, I popped into a small theater where 30 Slovenes (from a part of the former Yugoslavia that avoided the terrible destruction of the war) were watching a short film about the Old Bridge, its destruction, and its rebuilding. The persistent shelling of the venerable bridge, so rich in symbolism, seemed to go on and on. The Slovenes knew the story well. But when the video reached the moment when the bridge finally fell, I heard a sad collective gasp. It reminded me of how Americans feel, even well after 9/11, when watching video of the World Trade Center disappearing into a column of ash. It helped me, if not feel, at least appreciate another country's pain.

At lunchtime, I stopped at a tiny grocery store, where I was happy to see a woman I had befriended the day before. She was a gorgeous person, sad to be living in a frustrating economy, and stiff with a piece of shrapnel in her back

Firsthand Accounts Make History Spring to Life

Learning from a local who actually lived through those horrible years made my Mostar visit a particularly rich experience. Thankful for the lessons I learned in Mostar, I considered the value of firsthand accounts in my travels over the years.

When I was a gawky 14-year-old, my parents took me to Europe. In a dusty village on the border of Austria and Hungary, a family friend introduced me to a sage old man with breadcrumbs in his cartoonish white handlebar moustache. As the man spread lard on rustic bread, he shared his eyewitness account of the assassination of Archduke Franz Ferdinand in 1914. I was thrilled by history as never before.

In Prague, my Czech friend Honza took me on the walk he had taken every night for a week in 1989 with 100,000 of his countrymen as they demanded freedom from their Soviet overlords. The walk culminated in front of a grand building, where Honza said, "Night after night we assembled here, pulled out our key chains, and

all jingled them at the president's window, saying, 'It's time for you to go now.' Then one night we gathered... and he was gone. We had won our freedom." Hearing Honza tell that story as we walked that same route drilled into me the jubilation of a small country winning its freedom.

My Norwegian uncle Thor gave me a similarly powerful experience in Oslo. Gazing at mosaic murals in the Oslo City Hall that celebrate the heroics of locals who stood strong against German occupation, Thor told me stories of growing up in a Nazi-ruled Norway. He woke up one morning to find his beloved royal family in exile and

A lard-eater with a big moustache made history fun for a 14-year-old future travel writer.

With a local guide, like Aziz in Morocco, you'll learn more than just where to get the best tea.

German soldiers on every corner. Norway's resistance fighters took to the snowy mountains, coordinating with brave townspeople smuggling children to safety. Even with the vastly stronger occupying force, Thor told how his country's national spirit remained strong until that glorious day when the king returned and Norwegian flags flew happily again. As Thor brought the mural to life, I wondered what I would do to win back a freedom lost.

In Northern Ireland, my guide Stephen was determined to make his country's struggles vivid. In Belfast, he introduced me to the Felons' Club—where membership is limited to those who've spent at least a year and a day in a British prison for political crimes. Hearing heroic stories of Irish resistance while sharing a Guinness with a celebrity felon gives you an affinity for their struggles. Walking the next day through the green-trimmed gravesites of his prison-mates who starved themselves to death for the cause of Irish

independence capped the experience powerfully.

El Salvador's history is so tragic and fascinating that anyone you talk to becomes a tour guide. My Salvadoran guides with the greatest impact were the "Mothers of the Disappeared," who told me their story while leafing through humble scrapbooks showing photographs of their sons' bodies—mutilated and decapitated. Learning of a cruel government's actions with those sad mothers left me with lifetime souvenirs: a cynicism about many governments (you can tell by their actions who they really represent) and an empathy for underdogs courageously standing up to their leaders when necessary.

Tourists can go to Prague, Norway, Ireland, and Central America and learn nothing of a people's struggles. Or they can seek out opportunities to connect with people (whether professional guides or accidental guides) who can share perspective-changing stories.

that doctors decided was safer left in. She made me a hearty ham sandwich and helped me gather the ingredients of what would be a fine picnic meal. Stooping to pick up items on shelves lower than she could bend to reach, I considered how this woman's life will be forever marred by that war.

The sentiment I hear from locals when I visit this region is, "I don't know how we could have been so stupid to wage that unnecessary war." I've never met anyone here who called the war anything but a tragic mistake. The lesson I learned from their mistake is the importance of taking pluralism within your society seriously. While Bosnian sectarianism is extreme, every society has groups that could come to blows. And failing to find a way to live peacefully together—as the people of Mostar learned—means everybody loses.

Smells like Bosnian teen spirit.

That night in Mostar, as the teenagers ripped it up at their dance halls, I lay in bed sorting out my impressions. Until the wee hours, a birthday party raged in the restaurant outside my window. For hours they sang songs. At first I was annoyed. Then I realized that a Bosniak "Beach Boys" party beats a night of shelling. In two hours of sing-alongs, everyone seemed to know all the words...and I didn't recognize a single tune. In spite of all its challenges and setbacks, I have no doubt that this Bosnian culture will rage on.

Cetinje: Monks, Track Suits, and Europe's Worst Piano

Leaving Mostar, I drove over patched mortar craters in the pavement. In Sarajevo, they've filled these scars with red concrete to make them memorials. They call them "Sarajevo roses." Here the roses were black like the rest of the street—but after my Mostar experience, they showed up red in my mind.

Circling back to Dubrovnik, I drove south to yet another new nation that emerged from the ashes of Yugoslavia: Montenegro. During my travels through this region, my punch-drunk passport would be stamped and stamped and stamped. While the unification of Europe has made most border crossings feel archaic, the breakup of Yugoslavia has kept them in vogue here. Every time the country splintered, another border was set up. The poorer the country, it seems, the more ornate the border formalities. And by European standards, Montenegro is about as poor as it gets. They don't even have their own currency. With just 600,000 people, they decided, heck, let's just use euros.

For me, Montenegro, whose name means "Black Mountain," has always evoked the fratricidal chaos of a bygone age. I think of a time when fathers in the Balkans taught their sons that "your neighbor's neighbor is your friend" in anticipation of future sectarian struggles. When, for generation after generation, so-and-so-ovich was pounding on so-and-so-ovich (in Slavic names, "-ovich" means "son," like Johnson), a mountain stronghold was worth the misery.

My recent visit showed me that this image is now dated, the country is on an upward trajectory, and many expect to see Montenegro emerging as a sunny new hotspot on the Adriatic coastline.

Most tourists stick to Montenegro's scenic and increasingly glitzy Bay of Kotor, where the Adriatic cuts into the steep mountains like a Norwegian fjord. But—inspired by my back-roads Bosnian experience—I was eager to get off the beaten path and headed deep into the rugged interior of the "Black Mountain."

A zigzag road leads high above the Bay of Kotor to the historic capital of Montenegro.

I climbed 25 switchbacks—someone painted numbers on each one—ascending from the Montenegrin coast with its breezy palm trees, popular ice cream stands, and romantic harbor promenades into a world of lonely goats, scrub brush, and remote, seemingly deserted farmhouses. At switchback #4, I passed a Gypsy encampment. At #18, I pulled out for a grand view of the Bay of Kotor and, pulling on my sweater, marveled at how the vegetation, climate, and ambience were completely different just a few twists in the road above sea level.

At #24, I noticed the "old road"—little more than an overgrown donkey path—that was once the mountain kingdom's umbilical cord to the Adriatic. The most vivid thing I remember about my last visit, decades ago, was that a grand piano had literally been carried up the mountain so some big-shot nobleman could let it go slowly out of tune in his palace.

As I crested the ridge, the sea disappeared and before me stretched a basin defined by a ring of black mountains—Montenegro's heartland. Exploring the poorest corner of any European country can be eye-opening—but Montenegro's is more evocative than most. Desolate farmhouses claim to sell smoked ham, mountain cheese, and *medovina* (honey brandy), but I didn't see a soul. Up here, the Cyrillic alphabet survives better than on the coast. Every hundred yards or so, the local towing company had spray-painted on a rock, "*Auto Slep* 067-838-555." You had a feeling they were in the bushes praying for a mishap. Pulling off for a photo of the valley, I noticed a plaque marking where Tito's trade minister was assassinated in a 1948 ambush. At the end of the road was Cetinje, which the road sign proclaimed as the "Old Royal Capital." I'm nostalgic about this town, a classic mountain kingdom (with that grotesquely out-of-tune grand piano) established as the capital in the 15th century. Cetinje was taken by the Ottomans several times. The rampaging Ottomans would generally move in and enjoy a little raping, pillaging, and plundering. But, quickly realizing there was little hedonism to enjoy in Cetinje, they basically just destroyed the place and moved out. With the way clear, the rugged and determined residents filtered back into the ruins of their town and rebuilt.

Today Cetinje is a workaday, two-story town with barely a hint of its old royal status. The museums are generally closed. The economy is flat. A shoe factory and a refrigerator factory were abandoned with Yugoslavia's breakup. (They were part of Tito's economic vision for Yugoslavia—where, in the name of efficiency, individual products were made in one place in huge quantities to supply the entire country.) Kids on bikes rolled like tumbleweeds down the main street past old-timers with hard memories.

At the edge of town is the St. Peter of Cetinje Orthodox monastery— the still-beating spiritual heart of the country. I stepped in. An Orthodox monk—black robe and beard halfway to his waist—nodded a welcome. A service was in progress. Flames flickered on gilded icons, incense created an otherworldly ambience, and the chanting was almost hypnotic.

I stood (as everyone does in Orthodox worship) in the back. People— mostly teenagers in sporty track suits—were trickling in...kissing everything in sight. Seeing these rough and casual teens bending respectfully at the waist as they kissed icons, bibles, and the hands of monks was mesmerizing. If you saw them on the streets, you'd never dream that they'd be here standing through a long Orthodox service.

For the first time I understood what the iconostasis (called a "rood screen" in Western Europe) is all about. Used long ago in Catholic churches, and still today in Orthodox churches, the screen separates the common worshippers from the zone where the priests do all the religious "heavy lifting." Behind the screen—which, like a holy lattice, provides privacy but still lets you peek through—I could see busy priests in fancy robes, and above it all the outstretched arms of Jesus. I knew he was on the cross, but I only saw his arms. As the candlelight flickered, I felt they were happy arms... wanting and eager to give everyone present a big, Slavic bear hug.

Standing through an Eastern Orthodox service there, in a humble church in the forgotten historic capital of a mountain kingdom, I was thankful I had zigzagged to that remote corner of Europe. All those switchbacks earned me the chance to witness a vibrant and time-honored tradition surviving the storms of globalization and modernization.

From Cetinje, I descended back to the Bay of Kotor. At the humble waterfront town of Perast, young guys in swim trunks edged their boats near the dock, jockeying to motor tourists out to the island in the middle of the bay. According to legend, fishermen saw the Virgin Mary in the reef and began a ritual of dropping a stone on the spot every time they sailed by. Eventually the island we see today was created, and upon that island the people built a fine little church.

I hired a guy with a dinghy to ferry me out and was met by a young woman who gave me a tour. In the sacristy hung a piece of embroidery—a 25-year-long labor of love made by a local parishioner 200 years ago. It was

Montenegro's Bay of Kotor rewards the curious traveler.

as exquisite as possible, lovingly made with the finest materials available: silk and the woman's own hair. I could trace her laborious progress through the line of cherubs that ornamented the border. As the years went by, the hair of the angels (like the hair of the devout artist) turned from dark brown to white. Humble and anonymous as she was, she had faith that her work was worthwhile and would be appreciated—as it is, two centuries later, by a steady parade of travelers from distant lands.

I've been at my work for over 25 years now. I also have a faith that it (my work, if not my hair) will be appreciated. That's perhaps less humble than the woman was, but her work reassured me that we live on through our deeds. Her devotion to her creation (as well as to her creator) is an inspiration to do both good and lasting work. While traveling, I'm often struck by how people give meaning to life by producing and contributing.

I didn't take a photograph of the embroidery. For some reason, I didn't even take notes. At the moment, I didn't realize I was experiencing the highlight of my day. The impression of the woman's tenderly created embroidery needed—like a good red wine—time to breathe. That was a lesson for me. I was already mentally on to the next thing. When the power of the impression opened up, it was rich and full-bodied...but I was long gone. If travel is going to have the impact on you that it should, you have to climb into those little dinghies and reach for those experiences—the best ones won't come to you. And you have to let them breathe.

Back in town, I had a *bela kava* ("white coffee," as a latte is called here) and watched kids coming home from school. Two older girls walked by happily spinning the same kind of batons my sisters spun when I was a tyke. And then a sweet younger girl walked by all alone—lost in thought, carrying a tattered violin case.

Even in a country without its own currency, in a land where humble is everything's middle name, parents can find an old violin and manage to give their little girls grace and culture. Letting that impression breathe, it made me happier than I imagined it would.

Traveling in war-torn former Yugoslavia, I see how little triumphs can be big ones. I see hardscrabble nations with big aspirations. And I see the value of history in understanding our travels, and the value of travel in understanding our history.

Chapter 3
Europe Unites: Successes and Struggles

While I dabble in the rest of the world, my true love is Europe. Since my first trip there in 1969, I've enjoyed gaining an appreciation for Europe's history, art, culture, cuisine, music...and politics.

The big news in Europe these days is unification. Hosting two world wars within one lifetime inspired European nations to understand the necessity of working together. With the advent of the European Union (EU), its 27 (and counting) member nations have succeeded in attaining their two key goals: avoiding intra-European war and integrating their economies. Now they're moving on to new challenges: forming a common foreign policy and an integrated legal system. Of course, it's dangerous to generalize about "Europe," and many Europeans are not in step with the EU. These "Euroskeptics" mock the EU's high-minded ideals in light of its obvious failings. But despite foot-dragging in certain quarters, Europe as a whole is moving forward.

Europe is the part of the world most similar to the USA. That's why I consider it the wading pool for world exploration. Americans and Europeans are both affluent, well-educated peoples who love their freedom. But, while we have much in common, we also have fundamental differences. I learn a lot about America by studying Europe. Europe does some things better than we do. Some things, they do worse. And most things are open to debate. Europe doesn't have all the answers. But neither do we. Considering innovative European approaches to persistent challenges that vex our own nation can be constructive. This chapter assembles a few of my favorite examples.

Europe's "Big Government":
High Taxes with High Expectations

While Europe has its share of economic woes, there's no denying that Europeans have created a vast free trade zone that's designed to keep the Continent competitive with the United States and the emerging economic giants of

The Old World comes with a youthful energy.

China and India. With the unification of Europe, hundreds of millions of people now have the same euro coins jingling in their pockets...and the value of those euros has risen.

While in past years it seems Americans have been given two options (big, bad government or little, good government), Europeans are more likely to strive for a third option: big, good government.

In American politics, "socialism" is often perceived as an all-or-none bogeyman, evoking the stifling Soviet system of the Cold War. This thinking, which fixates on a Stalin-style oppression that has nothing to do with today's European socialism, ignores the reality that socialism is a spectrum. Every society on earth—including our own—includes some socialistic elements (such as our progressive taxation).

Like us, Europe is enthusiastically capitalistic. Europeans are just more comfortable with a higher degree of socialism. Most Europeans continue to favor their existing high tax rates because they believe that collectively creating the society of their dreams is more important than allowing individuals to create the personal empire of their dreams.

While American culture tends to be individualistic—inspired by "up by the bootstraps" and "rags to riches" stories—Europe is more focused on community. While we are more religious, Europe is more humanistic. In Scandinavia—the most highly taxed, socialistic, and humanistic corner of Europe—you don't find a church with a spire on the main square. You find a city hall with a bell tower. Inside, a secular nave leads not to a pulpit, but to a lectern. Behind that lectern, a grand mosaic tells epic stories—not from the Bible, but celebrating heroic individuals who contributed mightily to their community.

Europeans pay high taxes to buy big, good government...and expect results. Those results include an extensive social-welfare network that puts the financial burden of childcare, healthcare, education, and retirement on the collective shoulders of society, rather than on individuals. I once asked Olle, my Swiss friend, "How can you Swiss people be so docile about paying such high taxes?" Without missing a beat, he replied, "Well, what's it worth to live in a society where there is no homelessness, no hunger, and where everybody enjoys equal access to quality healthcare and education?"

The benefits are everywhere. A Slovenian friend of mine who had a baby was guaranteed a year's maternity leave at near-full pay...and was given a state-subsidized "starter kit" with all the essential gear she needed to care for her newborn. If anyone (even a foreign traveler) goes to a public hospital for urgent care in Europe, they often won't even see the bill. Higher education in Europe is subsidized. In many countries, it's entirely free, and students even get "pocket money" while they are learning. Hundreds of thousands of students and professors have traveled to other EU countries to study, teach, and build a sprawling network of intra-European relations through the EU-funded Erasmus Program.

Olle and Maria pay high taxes with high expectations... high in the Alps.

Don't get me wrong. Most Europeans grumble about paying sky-high taxes as much as anyone, and tax evasion is a national pastime for many. But philosophically, they understand that when it comes to taxes, the necessity outweighs the evil. European politicians don't have to promise tax cuts to win elections. As of this writing, the president of Finland, Tarja Kaarina, was well into her second six-year term leading one of the most highly taxed countries in Europe, and she had about a 75 percent approval rating. Like many Europeans, Finns support high taxes and big government because they like what they get in return.

A flipside of this system is that Europe doesn't have the ethic of individual charitable giving that we have in the US. We go to auctions and bake sales to support a good cause. We help our children raise money to subsidize school projects. Our local orchestras wouldn't exist without financial gifts from donors committed to that slice of culture. And public television is only possible with generous support from viewers like you. You don't see that so

much in Europe. Europeans expect
the government to care for the needy
and fund the arts, youth groups, and
foreign study opportunities. Europe's
tax-funded alternative to charity auctions, pledge drives, and school car
washes works for them.

In our system, the thinking is
that, after we all get wealthy, we'll be
sure to make charitable contributions
to the places where the fabric of our
society is frayed. But Europe is more
socialistic. Rather than a thousand
points of light emanating from generous community members who care,
Europeans prefer one compassionate, well-organized searchlight from
their entire society as orchestrated

In Stockholm, like elsewhere in humanistic
Scandinavia, the city hall's bell tower rather
than a church spire marks the center of
town.

by elected officials. While we care individually, they care collectively. What's
perceived as good for the fabric of their community (such as having bike
lanes, heroin maintenance clinics, public broadcasting, after-school childcare
for working parents, paid maternity and paternity leave, and freeway art)
trumps business interests.

This represents another major philosophical difference. In America we
believe in government by and for the people through the corporations that
we own. We want to have a good business environment so we can all share
in the affluence. I was raised with the business mantra, "What's good for GM
is good for America."

Europeans strive for government by the people and for the people sometimes *regardless* of the interests of their corporations. Consequently, Europe
is willing to make laws that are (at least in the narrow view) bad for business.
While in Europe, the notion of paying for a car's disposal when you first buy
the car makes sense, it would be dismissed in the US as bad for the economy.
Because carbon taxes would be considered good for the environment but bad
for business, I expect to see them in Europe before the US.

Even as Europeans accept this system, they love to complain about the
heavy-handedness of big government. Cumbersome bureaucracy creeps into

European Solutions

Throughout the world, people solve similar problems with different approaches. Here are some European answers.

① All my life, I've paid the city for a sanitation worker to pick up my garbage. In Switzerland, the garbage bag costs more...and includes pick-up. When it's full, put it out on any curb. The next morning, it's gone. ② An Italian law requires drivers to wear a seatbelt. Your car makes annoying noises if you don't buckle up. So the Italians, in their own creative way, have designed a handy little plug to quiet their car. *Problema finito*. ③ Junk mail exasperates us. Others don't like junk mail, either. Many Europeans have a simple solution. They put a decal on the mailbox that says simply "no" or "yes" to different types of junk mail. ④ While we have stop signs in the middle of nowhere, the British have roundabouts. You don't stop. You wing into that roundabout and take off at the exit of your choice. ⑤ In the Netherlands, they have four-story parking garages for bicycles. The Dutch take the train in, hop on their bike, and pedal to work. It's not necessarily out of dedication to the environment. Biking simply works well.

virtually all aspects of life. Strict health codes for restaurants dictate that cooked food must be frozen if it's not served within three hours. My Czech friend complained, "This makes many of our best dishes illegal." (Czech specialties, often simmered, taste better the next day.) A Polish farmer I know gripes that, when Poland joined the EU, he had to get "passports" for his cows. Italians chafed at having to wear helmets while riding their otherwise stylish *motorinos*. Throughout the EU, people are compromising as one-size-fits-all governance takes a toll on some of their particular passions.

While Europeans seem to find clever ways to get government on their backs, the American chorus has long been, "Get the government off our backs." We don't want regulations—especially the extreme examples cited above. While the financial crisis that erupted in 2008 brought attention to the problematic lack of regulations on both sides of the Atlantic, America has long had a less regulated business environment than Europe.

On the other hand, in Europe, workers' protection, environmental protection, and what seems like an obsession for regulations in general make even surviving as a small employer tough. Europe is a challenging, even demoralizing environment for running a small business. While I appreciate the way Europe organizes much of its society, I'm thankful I run my business here rather than there. In Europe, I could never have the creative fun I enjoy as an entrepreneur in the USA.

Is the American approach "wrong" and Europe's approach "right?" As a taxpayer and a businessman, I see pros and cons to both systems. We can all benefit by comparing notes.

Europeans Work Less

One priority of the European approach is striking a comfortable work-life balance. The EU has about 500 million people, with an annual economy of around 13 trillion dollars. To put that into relative terms, the United States, with 300 million people, has an economy of approximately the same size. Proponents of the American system point out that Europeans don't make as much money as we do. It's true—with more people generating only the same gross economy, they earn less per person. But Western European workers make essentially the same per hour as ours do. They just choose to work fewer hours.

I was raised believing there was one good work ethic: You work hard. While we call this *the* work ethic, it's actually only *a* work ethic. Europeans have a different one. They choose to work roughly 25 percent fewer hours

European adults get lots of time to play.

and willingly make roughly 25 percent less money. While this may not be good for business, it is good for life. Choosing to work less is part of "family values" in Europe; meanwhile, here in business-friendly America, working less is frowned upon…almost subversive.

A Greek friend of mine spent twenty years working in New York. Only after he retired and returned to Greece did he realize that not once in all those years in America did he take a nap. Back in Greece, if he's sleepy in the afternoon, he takes a snooze. Europeans marvel at how Americans seem willing, almost eager, to work themselves into an early grave. In many countries, European friends have told me proudly, "We don't live to work… we work to live."

Europeans understand the trade-off. Because they choose to work less, most Europeans don't strive for the material affluence that their American counterparts do. European housing, cars, gadgets, and other "stuff" are modest compared to what an American with a similar job might own. It's a matter of priorities. Just as Europeans willingly pay higher taxes for a higher standard of service, they choose less pay (and less stuff) in exchange for more time off. Imagine this in your own life: Would you make do with a smaller car if you knew you didn't have to pay health insurance premiums and co-pays? Would you be willing to give up the luxury of a big flat-screen TV and live in a smaller house if you could cut back to 35 hours per workweek and get a few extra weeks of paid vacation? For most Americans, I imagine that the European idea of spending more time on vacation and with their family, instead of putting in hours of overtime, is appealing.

I have an American friend who runs a very small movement called Take Back Your Time (www.timeday.org). Its mission: to teach Americans that we have the shortest vacations in the rich world, and it's getting worse. His movement's national holiday is October 24th. That's because, by its estimates, if we accepted only the typical European workload, yet worked as long and hard as people do in the US, October 24th would be the last day of the year we'd have to go to work.

With the pressures of globalization, Europe is having to rethink some of its "live more, work less" ideals. For example, the Spanish government is funding incentives to keep workers from going home for a midday siesta, which most agree hurts productivity. And I have a theory that in Ireland (where sales of Guinness are down), the number of pubs is shrinking at the same rate that the number of cafés is increasing, because that society is ramping up its productivity. Drinkers of heavy stout are shifting to lighter lagers, and drinkers of lager are shifting to coffee. Replacing beer with caffeine is a symptom of our faster-paced, more competitive world.

Europe's Internal Marshall Plan

Europe is dedicated to bringing its infrastructure up to snuff. After World War II, the United States invested in rebuilding Europe with the Marshall Plan. It was a smart policy designed to assure us strong and stable trading partners and allies. Recently, for essentially the same reasons, Europe has employed a kind of internal Marshall Plan—investing in roads, rail lines, communication, education, and other improvements to strengthen their union.

When a nation joins the European Union, it's either a "net contributor" or a "net receiver." While there's lots of wrangling in Brussels about just who gives and gets what, Europeans know their economic union is only as strong as its weakest link. Therefore, wealthy countries give more than they get—willingly, if not always enthusiastically. That money bolsters the poorer countries until they develop to the point where, rather than weak links, they become net contributors as well.

Europe (led by France and Germany) is investing hundreds of billions of euros to build a transportation and communication infrastructure for the future. Travelers not only see this, they benefit from it.

Among the original members of the European Union, Portugal, Greece, and Ireland were the net receivers. Back then, I remember no freeways in any of those countries. Now they're rolling out freeways in all of them. And every time you drive on a slick new thoroughfare, you see a European flag reminding locals where the funding came from.

The Cost of Policing the World

While it's easy for pacifists (at home and abroad) to complain about the US military, the reality is that we are the world's traffic cop. Americans pay with blood and money to protect victims of tyranny and to defend democracy and free enterprise around the world. Defeating the USSR, saving people from genocide in Kosovo, deposing a dictator in Iraq, and fighting the Taliban in Afghanistan are expensive. Typically, the US foots most of the bill while Europe moves in with peacekeeping forces afterwards. Or, as some people put it, "The US does the cooking, and Europe does the dishes."

Given America's unique world-leadership position, our limited economic means, and the world's reliance on our military might, we need to choose our battles thoughtfully. There are cases where the world supports our involvement (Darfur, Kosovo, Afghanistan), and places where they don't (Central America and Iraq). We can do whatever we want...but it sure makes things easier on everybody when we wield our might with the support of our friends and allies.

Perhaps the EU wouldn't have so much money for its infrastructure if it had to do its own fighting. But consider the flipside: By their judgment, sinking money into their infrastructure rather than into their military is better for their long-term security. In the European view, America is trapped in an inescapable cycle to feed its military-industrial complex: As we bulk up our military, we look for opportunities to make use of it. (When your only tool is a hammer, you treat every problem like a nail.) And then, when we employ our military unwisely, we create more enemies...which makes us feel the need to grow our military even more. If an American diplomat complained to his European counterpart, "America is doing all the heavy lifting when it comes to military," the European might respond, "Well, you seem to be enjoying it. We're building roads and bridges instead."

Traveling affords a good opportunity to consider how American military might has helped make our world a better place—and how it hasn't—and what kind of fiscal and military policies make a society stronger and safer.

Europe's new high-speed train network is good for commerce...but bad for birds.

Trains are faster than ever. On a recent visit to Munich, I was photographing trains pulling in to the station—with birds squished onto the windshields. Looking at those poor birds, I thought, "You'd wait all your life to see a bird squished onto a windshield of a train back in my hometown."

A bullet train now zips under the English Channel, taking people from Paris to London in two and a half hours. Denmark and Sweden built a mammoth bridge connecting Copenhagen and Malmö, creating Scandinavia's largest metropolitan area. And cities throughout Europe seem to be forever dug up because they are constantly improving and expanding their underground transit systems.

Non-EU nations are investing, too. Norway, with fewer than five million people, is drilling some of the longest tunnels in the world to lace together isolated communities in the fjords. Istanbul has scraped together the money to build a massive train tunnel under the Bosphorus to connect Asia and Europe and grease its economic engine. And there's an effort underway to dig a tunnel connecting Spain and Morocco under the Strait of Gibraltar.

Savvy nations understand that infrastructure is the foundation for prosperity (and power). Hitler knew he couldn't take on Europe without a good highway system, so he built the autobahn. The United States undertook a massive investment in our interstate highway system in the 1950s, which helped our country truck itself into greater economic power. And in our generation, Europe is investing money it could be spending on its military on its infrastructure instead.

Exploring a continent with a level of affluence similar to the US's gives us a chance to see firsthand the result of allocating limited resources with different priorities. People everywhere

Berlin's new train station is the biggest in Europe, with 1,800 trains a day arriving on 14 major train lines, coming in at right angles on two different levels.

hear the excuse "there's not enough money." In actuality, there *is* enough money... just different priorities. New stadium, healthcare for all, faster trains, extravagant cathedral, subsidized education, tax cuts, next-generation bomber...each society makes different choices according to its priorities.

Europe Wants Peace

So far I've focused on the economy of the European Union. But for the EU's founders, money took a backseat to their primary motivation: peace. Even the biggest Euroskeptic recognizes that, in weaving together the economies of former enemies like France and Germany, everyone has become so interconnected that Europe will never again suffer devastation from a major war as they did twice in the last century. The French and the Germans still don't agree on most things. But now they've become too financially interdependent to take up arms over their differences. Minimizing the possibility of an intra-European war is *the* triumph of the EU.

When boots do hit the ground in a war, Europeans believe it's because they have failed to prevent it. They prefer endless diplomacy to once-in-a-while war. Europe's reluctance to go to war frustrates some Americans. I believe their relative pacifism is because Europeans know the reality of war, while most Americans do not. Of course, if you have a loved one who has fought or died in Iraq, Afghanistan, or Vietnam, you know what a war is. But as a society, the US can't remember actually hosting a war. Europeans have told me that they believe Americans were more willing to use cluster bombs and napalm to pacify Fallujah because in the age of modern warfare, no American city has ever been wiped from existence like Coventry, Dresden, Rotterdam, or Warsaw. It's easier to feel detached when a war is something you watch on the nightly news, rather than something that killed your grandfather or destroyed your hometown.

Europe knows what a war is. It ripped itself to shreds twice within my grandparents' lifetime. Consider France in World War I. France (with one-quarter as many people as we have) lost as many people as we've lost in the entire Iraq War—over 4,000 people—in one day...many times. They lost as many people as we lost in Vietnam (60,000) in one month. And then it happened again and again until, by the end of World War I, an estimated half of all the men in France between the ages of 15 and 30 were casualties. When some Americans, frustrated at France's reluctance to follow us into a war, call the French "surrender monkeys," I believe it shows their ignorance of history.

If there is a national piece of art today for the European Union, it is Picasso's *Guernica*, because it reminds Europe of the reality of war.

After World War I, Europe was awakening to the destructive power of aerial bombardments. During the Spanish Civil War in 1937, Hitler jumped at a chance to help his fellow fascist, General Francisco Franco, by bombing the Basque town of Guernica. Surveying the rubble of that town made it clear that technology had taken the destructive power of war to new heights. This inspired Picasso to create his greatest work. His mural *Guernica* memorialized the first city destroyed by an aerial bombardment and gave Europe a preview of the horrors of its fast-approaching war with frightening accuracy.

In 1947, in the rubble of a bombed-out Europe, Euro-visionaries assembled and agreed that they needed to overcome the hell that they were bringing upon themselves every couple of generations with these wars. Their solution was to unite. Of course, a union is nothing without people giving up some measure of real sovereignty. Since 1947, proponents of a European Union have been convincing the people of proud and independent nations to trade away bits and pieces of their independence. It's a tough sell. But in a fitful evolution—two steps forward and one step back—over the last sixty or so years, they have created a European union.

Fewer Borders, but More Ethnic Diversity

A key strategy for preserving peace in a sprawling, multiethnic state is to respect and celebrate diversity. As if inspired by America's *e pluribis unum* ("out of many, one"), the European Union's official motto is *in varietate concordia* ("united in diversity").

I'm charmed by Europe's ethnic diversity. Hop on a train for two hours and you step out into a different culture, different language, and different heritage. As I watched Europe unite, I (like many of my European friends) feared that this diversity would be threatened. But just the opposite is happening.

In today's Europe, there are three loyalties: region, nation, and Europe. Ask a person from Munich where he's from, and he'll say, "I'm Bavarian," or "I'm German," or "I'm European," depending on his generation and his outlook. Ask somebody from Barcelona, and she'll say, "I'm Catalan," or "I'm Spanish," or "I'm European."

Borders and loyalties can be messy. Modern political borders are rarely clean when it comes to dividing ethnic groups. And most of the terrorism and troubles in Europe—whether Basque, Irish, Catalan, or Corsican—have been about ethnic-minority separatist movements threatening national capitals. Appreciating the needs of these people, peace-loving European leaders strive to make the Continent's minority groups feel like they belong.

As Europe unites, established countries are less threatened by "nations without states." In 1999, Scotland convened a parliament in Scotland for the first time since 1707...and London didn't stop them.

Brittany, in western France, is not ethnically French. People there are Celtic, cousins of the Welsh and the Irish. Just a couple of generations ago, Paris was so threatened by the secessionist dreams of these Celts that if parents gave their newborn a Celtic name, that child would not be granted a French national identity card. Such a policy would be laughable today.

When I first visited Barcelona in the 1970s, locals weren't allowed to speak Catalan or dance their beloved Sardana. The Catalan flag was outlawed, so locals waved the flag of the Barcelona soccer team instead. Now, in public schools, children speak Catalan first, local flags fly proudly, and every Sunday in front of the cathedral, people gather to dance the Sardana. This circle dance symbolizes national unity as all differences are cast aside

This Tirolean archaeologist funds his vision with money from Brussels.

and Catalans raise their hands together to proudly celebrate their ethnicity. A Catalan person in Barcelona told me, "Catalunya is Spain's Quebec. We don't like people calling our corner of Iberia a 'region' of Spain...because that's what Franco called it. We do not accept subjugation as a region of Spain. We are a nation without a state."

What's going on? Barcelona is less threatening to Madrid. Edinburgh doesn't scare London. Brittany gets along with Paris (and I don't mean Spears and Hilton). As power shifts to the EU capital of Brussels, national capitals recognize and accept that their authority is waning. And the European Union supports transnational groups in the hopes of reminding big nations that they have more in common than they might realize.

A friend of mine, Armin Walch, is the "Indiana Jones" of Tirolean archaeologists. When Armin wants money to excavate a castle, he goes to Brussels. If he says, "I'm doing something for Austria," he'll go home empty-handed. So instead, he says he's doing something for the Tirol (an ethnic region that spans parts of Italy and Austria, ignoring the modern national boundary)... and gets funding.

Europe's "stateless nations" live in solidarity with each other. The Catalan people find Basque or Galician bars a little more appealing than the run-of-the-mill Spanish ones. They even make a point to include the other languages on their ATMs: In Barcelona, you'll see Catalan first, then Spanish, Galego

Europe Spreads East

On May 1, 2004, eight formerly communist nations joined the European Union...and suddenly the EU grew by 75 million people. In 2007, two more Soviet Bloc additions boosted the population by another 30 million. In just a few short years, the geographical center of Europe shifted from Brussels to Prague.

Eastern Europe is changing fast. Freedom is old news, communism is a distant memory, and they have long settled into the grind of capitalism. In the 1990s, societies once forced to espouse Soviet economics embraced the capitalist work ethic with gusto— as if making up for lost time. While adjusting from the security of a totalitarian system to the insecurity of freedom, my friends there reported that younger and better-educated people jumped at this opportunity to get ahead—working longer hours, having fewer children, and buying more cars. On the other hand, older people missed the job security and sense of safety while walking down the streets that they remember from the "good old, bad old days." And many less-educated young people who see the new system working against them joined angry and racist groups such as eastern Germany's skinheads. Now in the 21st century, more of capitalism's realities, limits, and frustrations are sinking in.

I remember visits to the Eastern Bloc during the Cold War. Back then life was bleak, gray, and demoralizing because of ongoing political repression and their unresponsive Soviet-style command economy. Someone would dictate how many of these and how much of that would be produced, ignoring the basic laws of supply and demand. It was a fiasco. On my early visits to Poland, people were taking their windshield wipers in with them at night. The government under-produced wipers, and the thieves knew it. They'd rip off somebody's wipers and sell them for a fortune on the black market.

But Eastern Europe has put itself on a fast track to catch up with the West. Today, with a solid supply-

Eastern Europe is enjoying freedom and a new affluence.

and-demand economy, the Poles are leaving their windshield wipers on their cars at night. Compared to the 1980s, Eastern Europe feels like a festival of pent-up entrepreneurial spirit. And for me, each visit is a case study in the fundamental wisdom of free enterprise and the laws of supply and demand.

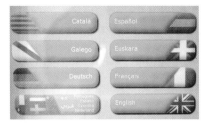

Language options on an ATM show solidarity among smaller ethnic groups.

(the language of Galicia, in northwest Spain), Euskara (the Basque tongue), and then German, French, English... and a button for all the rest. While all of these groups—Catalan, Galician, and Basque—speak the common language of Spanish, they respect each other's native tongues as a way to honor their shared ethnic-underdog status.

These groups' affinity for each other even factors into where they travel. On a recent trip to Northern Ireland, I was impressed by how many travelers I met from Basque Country and Catalunya. Because the Basques and Catalans feel a kinship with the Catholic minority in Ireland's Protestant North, they choose to vacation in Ulster.

Europe is burdened with the image of a too-politically-correct bureaucracy, notorious for dictating the proper curve of a cucumber in 23 official languages. But they don't mind the teasing. While attempting to honor the linguistic and idealistic wishes of its unruly gang of members isn't always efficient, Europe understands that watching out for its ethnic underdogs is essential for maintaining its hard-won peace.

Planting People Brings a Painful Harvest

In some cases, minority groups didn't wind up where they are by choice, but were "planted." While the world is filled with struggling minority groups who stand in solidarity with each other, groups of people sent as settlers by dominant cultures to establish their control over disputed land also have hardships and feel a related solidarity for each other. For instance, I saw Israeli flags flying from flag posts in Protestant communities all over Northern Ireland. Ulster and Israeli settlers empathize with each other. Protestants "planted" in the 17th century by a bigger power (England) in Ulster are having a tough

Israeli flags fly next to the Union Jack in Northern Ireland, because settlers empathize with each other's struggles.

time with their indigenous neighbors. And Israeli settlers, planted by their government in land Palestinians claim, are having a tough time with their indigenous neighbors as well.

This is a story repeated time and again through history. During difficult times, military families from Soviet Russia retired in relative comfort in little Estonia. Today Estonia—now independent—struggles with a big Russian minority that refuses to integrate.

In the 16th century, the Habsburg monarchy planted Serbs—who were escaping from the Ottomans farther south—along the Croatian-Bosnian border, to provide a "human shield" against those same Ottomans. Many centuries later, descendants of those Serbian settlers and the indigenous Croats were embroiled in some of the bloodiest fighting of the war following the breakup of Yugoslavia.

Back when Britain ruled Ceylon (present-day Sri Lanka) and used it as a big tea plantation, they couldn't get the local Sinhalese to pick the tea cheaply enough, so they imported Tamils from India (who were more desperate and willing to work for less). When colonial rule became more trouble than the tea was worth, the Brits gave the island its freedom. And today, thanks to England's love of tea, the Sinhalese and Tamils are locked in a tragic civil war.

When I consider the problems that come with planting Jews in Palestine, Protestants in Ireland, Russians in Estonia, Serbs in Croatia, and Tamils in Sinhalese Sri Lanka, I'm impressed both by the spine of the people who were there first and the hardship borne by the ancestors of the original settlers. When observing this sort of sectarian strife, travelers see that when people from one land displace others from their historic homeland—regardless of the rationale or justification—a harsh lesson is learned. Too often the resulting pain (which can last for so many centuries that many even forget its roots) is far greater for all involved than the short-term gain for the powers doing the planting.

European Challenges: An Aging Continent Grapples with Immigration

I am a Europhile. I freely admit I have a romantic fascination with Europe and an appreciation for its way of life. But I'm not blind to the fact that Europe has its character flaws and is grappling—not always very well—with some serious challenges of its own.

As the birthrate has dropped in recent years, Europe is becoming a geriatric continent. While this is not a problem in itself, Europe's luxurious cradle-to-grave welfare system is only sustainable with more active workers and fewer retirees. People who worked all their lives with the promise of the cushy old-age benefits their parents enjoyed won't docilely accept the harsh reality as dictated by the new arithmetic. As in the USA, it's difficult to take away expected entitlements without a fight. Europeans love to demonstrate. And as courageous politicians try to make cuts to address the emerging crisis, there will be plenty of angry marches clogging Europe's grand boulevards.

Interestingly, as Europe's native population declines, its population growth may come largely from immigrants. And Europe's immigration challenges are much like America's. Around the world, rich nations import poor immigrants to do their dirty work. If a society doesn't want to pay for expensive apples picked by rich kids at high wages, it gets cheaper apples by hiring people willing to work for less. If you're wealthy enough to hire an immigrant to clean your house, you do it—you get a clean house, and the immigrant earns a wage. That's just the honest reality of capitalism.

When European workers lose entitlements, they hit the streets.

In Europe, *Gastarbeiter*—German for "guest worker"—is the generic term for this situation because Germans so famously imported Turkish people to do their scut work a generation ago, when Germany's post-WWII economic boom finally kicked into gear. These days, virtually every country in Western Europe has its own *Gastarbeiter* contingent. Berlin—with over 100,000 Turks—could be considered a sizable "Turkish city." France's population includes millions of poor North Africans. And even newly wealthy Ireland now has 100,000 Polish people taking out its trash. It's striking to hear my Irish friends speak about their new Polish worker as if he or she were a new appliance.

But invariably, wealthy people begin to realize that their "cheap labor" is not quite as cheap as they hoped. In Europe, the importation of labor creates fast-growing immigrant communities that need help and incentives to assimilate, or society at large will pay a steep price (as we saw in 2005, when the deaths of two black teenagers while being pursued by French cops ignited violent riots that rocked the poor African and Arab suburbs of Paris).

In Europe, many immigrants melt into their adopted homelands, while others flat-out don't want to assimilate. With the increasing affordability of modern communication technologies, it's becoming easier and easier for immigrants to establish insulated satellite communities that remain in constant contact with the culture and language of their homeland. When my grandparents migrated from Norway to the US, they effectively severed communications with their Norwegian relatives, and had little choice but to melt into American society. (And, while they arrived speaking barely a word of English, just two generations later, I barely speak a word of Norwegian.) Today they could use the Internet to read newspapers and watch television shows from home, and talk to relatives around the world for free on Skype.

These days, it seems that immigrant groups can choose whether or not they want to integrate with their adopted countries. I've met third-generation Algerians in the Netherlands who don't speak a word of Dutch, and don't expect their children to, either. And I've met third-generation Pakistanis in Denmark that speak only Danish and know and love their adopted new country just as their blonde neighbors do.

Like the US, Europe is suffering growing pains when it comes to its immigrants. Coming from an immigrant family in a nation of immigrants, I like America's "melting pot" approach. I think it works best for all if newcomers embrace their adopted culture, learn the local language, and melt in.

But the European scene is a bit more complex. While I'm a fan of melting in, I also respect the cultural diversity and survival of Europe's smaller ethnic groups. If diversity is such a virtue, what's wrong with immigrants wanting to preserve their home cultures? Is it hypocritical to celebrate the preservation of the Catalan language, but expect Algerians to learn Dutch? Should Europe's famous tolerance extend only to indigenous European cultures?

While I'm glad I'm not a policymaker who needs to implement immigration laws in Europe, I'll be honest about my take on this dicey issue: I favor indigenous diversity (policies favoring European "nations without states"), but policies facilitating immigrant laborers and their families (from outside Europe) to embrace local cultural norms and assimilate.

While Europe could probably learn more from America on immigration issues, as both societies grapple with this challenge, we can learn from each others' successes and failures.

The Tyranny of the Majority

Once, while riding the bus from Munich out to Dachau, I learned a lesson about the tyranny of the majority. En route to the infamous concentration camp memorial, I sat next to an old German woman. I smiled at her weakly as if to say, "I don't hold your people's genocidal atrocities against you." She glanced at me and sneered down at my camera. Suddenly, surprising me with her crusty but fluent English, she ripped into me. "You tourists come here not to learn, but to hate," she seethed.

Pulling the loose skin down from a long-ago-strong upper arm, she showed me a two-sided scar. "When I was a girl, a bullet cut straight through my arm," she said. "Another bullet killed my father. The war took many good people. My father ran a *Grüss Gott* shop."

I was stunned by her rage. But I sensed desperation on her part to simply unload her story on one of the hordes of tourists who tramp daily through her hometown to ogle at an icon of the Holocaust.

I asked, "What do you mean, a *Grüss Gott* shop?" She explained that in Bavaria, shopkeepers greet customers with a "*Grüss Gott*" ("May God greet you"). During the Third Reich, it was safer to change to the Nazi greeting, "*Sieg Heil*." It was a hard choice. Each shopkeeper had to make it. Everyone in Dachau knew which shops were *Grüss Gott* shops and which were *Sieg Heil* shops. Over time there were fewer and fewer *Grüss Gott* shops. Pausing, as if mustering the energy for one last sentence, she stood up and said, "My father's shop was a *Grüss Gott* shop to the end," then stepped off the bus.

Conflicts between the majority and the minority persist in today's Europe. Consider Northern Ireland, where the population is divided between Protestants (supporters of British rule) and Catholics (who identify with the Irish). While the familiar Union Jack of the UK is the "official" flag of Northern Ireland, minority Catholics who'd like to see Ireland united see it as a symbol of oppression. Unfortunately, they no longer consider it their flag, and call it "the Butcher's Apron" instead.

For a lesson in the power of symbolism, visit a town where about two-thirds of the community is Protestant and one-third is Catholic. These towns can be decked out like a Union Jack fantasy...or nightmare, if you happen to be Catholic. The curbs are painted red, white, and blue. Houses fly huge British flags. Streets lead under trellises blotting out the sky with flapping Union Jacks. (Not too long ago, many towns like these even came with the remains of a burned-out Catholic church.) A Catholic walking down a street strewn with this British symbolism can only be quiet and accept it. To independence-minded Catholics, the Union Jack symbolizes not a united nation, but the tyranny of the majority. The result: There is no real flag of Northern Ireland.

Until experiences like these in Germany and in Northern Ireland humanized the notion of "tyranny of the majority," I never really grasped the sadness of a society where a majority-rules mentality can, when

Many angry Catholics in Northern Ireland have no flag. To them, the Union Jack is "the Butcher's Apron."

taken to extremes, abuse a minority and bully it into silent submission.

As the rhetoric for the Iraq War was ramping up in early 2003, a situation in Edmonds, my hometown north of Seattle, reminded me in some small way of what I'd seen abroad. This was a difficult and emotional time, with all the patriotic fervor that comes with an invasion. Perhaps a third of our town opposed the war, and two-thirds supported it. The Lions Club lined the streets of our town with American flags and declared they would stay there in support of our troops until they finished the job and came home in victory.

While I supported our troops, I opposed the war because I believed that the president knowingly lied to get us there. When the Lions Club erected all those flags—which were normally reserved for patriotic holidays—I became very uncomfortable. I wanted to embrace my flag, but was put in a regrettable position that doing so would be tantamount to supporting the war. I felt as though my flag had been demoted from something that all Americans shared (regardless of their politics) to a promotional logo for a war I didn't believe in. I knew several Edmonds merchants agreed that our Stars and Stripes had been kidnapped. But in my conservative town, they feared not flying it would threaten their business. They felt frightened. Their predicament reminded me of those German shopkeepers who had to stop saying "*Grüss Gott.*" And my own town reminded me of those red, white, and blue-drenched towns in Ulster. Although to a far lesser degree, I felt that here in my hometown, a minority (of which I was a part) was also being oppressed by a tyranny of the majority. In defense of our flag, I had to act.

I explained my concerns to the president of the Lions Club. He understood and agreed to have his club take down the flags after a week. It didn't happen. So, humming "Yankee Doodle Dandy" to myself, I marched through town collecting and carefully stowing the flags. It was a small, symbolic, and perhaps overly righteous move on my part, motivated by what I considered patriotic concerns.

While some supported me, many were angry. I was shark bait on Seattle's right-wing radio talk shows for several days. But now, when my little town is a festival of Stars and Stripes on holidays like the Fourth of July, Presidents' Day, and Election Day, everybody can celebrate together because the flag flies for all of us—even the peaceniks.

Tolerance and the Futility of Legislating Morality

I'm hopeful that Europe can overcome the challenge of its new ethnic mix because of its proven track record for pluralism. While Europe has no shortage of closed-minded, knee-jerk opinions, most Europeans consider tolerance a virtue to be cultivated. At the leading edge of this thinking is the Netherlands. Historically, this corner of Europe saw some of the most devastating Catholics-versus-Protestants fighting in the religious wars following the Reformation. They learned to be inclusive, welcoming Jews when others wouldn't and providing refuge to religious refugees (such as our nation's Pilgrim founders). And, as a major maritime power during the Age of Discovery, the Netherlands became a gateway to Europe for emigrants and immigrants (and their ideas) to and from all over Asia, Africa, and the Americas. Based on lessons learned from their history, it seems the Dutch have made a conscious decision to tolerate alternative lifestyles.

When I'm in the Dutch town of Haarlem, I'm struck by the harmony and compromise people have worked out between tradition and modernity, virtuous lives and hedonistic vices, affluence and simplicity. People live well—but in small apartments, getting around by bike and public transit. While the frugal Dutch may keep the same old one-speed bike forever, they bring home new flowers every day. The typical resident commutes by

In Amsterdam's Red Light District, sex workers are unionized.

train to glassy skyscrapers to work for giant corporations in nearby office parks, but no skyscraper violates Haarlem's downtown cityscape, which is still dominated by elegant old gables and church spires. In Haarlem, the latest shopping malls hide behind Dutch Renaissance facades. Streets are clogged with café tables and beer-drinkers. The cathedral towers over the market square with its carillon ringing out its cheery melody as policemen stroll in pairs—looking more like they're on a date than on duty.

Two blocks behind the cathedral, a coffeeshop (a place that legally sells marijuana) is filled with just the right music and a stoned clientele. People, enjoying a particularly heavy strain of marijuana, stare at their rolling papers as if those crinkly critters are alive. Others are mesmerized by the bubbles in their bongs.

And down by the canal, a fairytale of cobbled lanes and charming houses gather around a quiet little church, creating a scene right out of a Vermeer painting. But this neighborhood is different. Lonely men, hands in pockets, stroll as they survey prostitutes who giggle and flirt from their red-lit windows.

While the USA is inclined to legislate morality on issues such as prostitution, gay rights, and drugs, much of Europe takes a different approach. While countries differ, the general European sentiment is not to make a law forcing someone to be what the majority considers "moral." Instead, European law tolerates "immoral" acts as long as they don't hurt someone else.

For example, few on either side of the Atlantic would argue that prostitution is a good thing. But in most of Europe, where many people recognize that you can't just wish it away with laws, prostitution is generally legal and regulated.

Of course, each country has its own laws...and quirks. German sex workers rent rooms in multi-story "Eros Towers." If a Greek prostitute gets married, she must give up her license to sell sex. Portuguese call girls can lose custody of their children. Dutch hookers have a union. In Iceland and Switzerland, while prostitution is legal, it is illegal for a third party to profit from the sale of sex. In general, the hope is that when a prostitute needs help and pushes her emergency button, a policeman rather than a pimp comes to her rescue.

While that's the ideal, it's not foolproof. There is still sex trafficking and abuse of women in the sex trade. But Europeans figure with their more progressive, creative, and pragmatic approach to what they consider a "victimless crime," they are minimizing violence, reducing the spread of AIDS and other diseases, and allowing sex workers a better life...all while generating some additional tax revenue.

In another example of European pragmatism, Europe's drinking age is typically lower than the US's. While no country in the world has a higher drinking age than America's, most European countries allow 16- or 18-year-olds to consume alcohol. European parents recognize that—no matter how fiercely they moralize against alcohol—their teens will drink. (Europeans puzzle over why 18-year-old Americans can marry, buy a gun, go to war, and vote...but not buy a can of beer.)

To celebrate their graduation, Scandinavian students drink while their parents do the driving.

Around the world, when kids graduate from high school, they party, get drunk, and some die on the roads. When traveling through Scandinavia in May and June, you'll see a creative solution to this problem: truckloads of drunk high-school graduates noisily enjoying a parent-sponsored bash. The parents hire a truck and provide a driver so none of the students need to drive. The kids decorate their party truck. Then the whooping and hollering grads parade through their towns from one family home to the next, where parents each host one stage of the progressive graduation kegger. Just about everyone gets drunk. But no one lies, and no one dies. While this makes perfect sense to Scandinavian parents, it would be a tough sell for American parents.

This is just one example of pragmatic harm reduction motivating drug policy in Europe. In some parts of Europe, a joint of marijuana causes about as much excitement as a can of beer. And the Continent's needle junkies are dealt with by nurses, counselors, and maintenance clinics more than by cops, judges, and prisons. (The European approach to drug policy is covered in greater length in Chapter 7.)

While there are still intolerant corners (especially in the East), many Europeans seem to pride themselves in an unflappable tolerance. I was recently at a gay pride parade in Berlin. The entire gay community was out, it seemed, doing its flamboyant

Europe takes civil rights to extremes. Even farm animals are guaranteed certain rights by law. In 2008, Switzerland granted new rights to animals, including banning the use of live bait by fishermen, the right for sheep and goats to have at least a visual contact with their fellows, and a legal right for pigs to shower after rolling in the mud.

best to share their particular love of life. The streets were lined with tens of thousands of straight and more conservative Germans. I happened to be observing from the curb surrounded by what seemed like an entire senior center out on a field trip. I was struck by how all the leather, sex toys, and delirious mooning from a long line of slow-moving flatbed trucks was seen simply as entertainment and a celebration of freedom. Try as they might, all that in-your-face gay hedonism couldn't shock the straight and elderly crowd of onlookers.

Perhaps Europe's inclination to be tolerant is rooted in the intolerance of its past. In the 16th century, they were burning Protestants for their beliefs. In the 18th century, they were drowning women who stepped out of line as witches. In the 20th century, Nazis were gassing Jews, Gypsies, and gay people. Now in the 21st century, Europe seems determined to get human rights, civil liberties, and tolerance issues right.

Instead of legislating morality, Europe legislates tolerance and human rights. Along with all the rights an American would expect, the in-the-works European constitution will include the right to work, food, and education. All will have the right not only to healthcare, but to preventative healthcare. In Europe, the "right to life" means no death penalty. Europeans will all have the right to the protection of personal data, the right to access any data that has been collected, and the right to have it rectified if it is inaccurate. Everyone will have the right to paid leave and paid parental leave. And all will have the right to join or form a trade union. When the proposed constitution was unveiled, Valéry Giscard d'Estaing (then-president of France) declared proudly that "of all the men and women in the world, it is the citizens of Europe who will have the most extensive rights." While the European Union was not ready for such far-ranging idealism and this constitution was voted down, the vision is not dead and all expect something similar to soon be passed into law.

While the US is not likely to embrace tolerance with the sweeping idealism of some Europeans, just knowing that reasonable people endeavor to respect human diversity, promote inclusivity, and champion human rights to this degree can be empowering. Once back home, you have the option of tailoring your personal version of the American Dream with similar ideals.

European Flesh and the American Prude

On a lighter note, let's take a closer look at Europe's relatively open relationship with their bodies and with sex. While not as high-minded as war and peace or taxation and social services, this is an aspect of the cultural divide that titillates any American traveler to Europe who's window-shopped a magazine kiosk, gone to a beach or park on a sunny day, or channel-surfed broadcast TV late at night.

Thinking through my recent travels, I recall many examples of Europe's different attitudes about sex: My Dutch friends had, on their coffee table, a graphic government-produced magazine promoting safe sex. I was sitting on the toilet at an airport in Poland and the cleaning lady asked me to lift my legs so she could sweep. I learned that I can measure the romantic appeal of scenic pull-outs along the Amalfi Coast drive by how many used condoms litter the asphalt. Soap ads on huge billboards overlooking major city intersections in Belgium show lathered-up breasts. The logo of a German travel publisher is a traveler on a tropical-paradise islet leaning up against its only palm tree, hands behind his head, reading a book that's supported by his erect penis. Preschoolers play naked in fountains in Norway. A busty porn star is elected to parliament in Italy. Coppertoned grandmothers in the south of France have no tan lines. The student tourist center in Copenhagen welcomes visitors with a bowl of free condoms at the info desk. Accountants in Munich fold their suits neatly on the grass as every inch of their body soaks up the sun while taking a lunch break in the park.

I'm not comfortable with all of this. During a construction industry convention in Barcelona, locals laughed that they actually had to bus in extra prostitutes from France. I find the crude sexual postcards on racks all over the Continent gross, the Benny Hill-style T&A that inundates TV throughout Mediterranean Europe boorish, and the topless models strewn across page three of so many British newspapers insulting to women. And I'll never forget the time my wife and I had to physically remove the TV from our children's hotel room in Austria after seeing a couple slamming away on channel 7 (and the hotelier looked at us like we were crazy).

Comparisons with America are striking. In our culture, a children's TV star is routed into obscurity after he's caught masturbating in an adult theater. A pop star dominates the news media for days after revealing part of her breast for a split-second during a football halftime show. During one particularly moralistic time, statues of classical goddesses gracing our nation's Capitol were robed to protect easily offended eyes.

An early edition of my art-for-travelers guidebook featured a camera-toting *David*—full frontal nudity, Michelangelo-style—on the cover. My publisher's sales reps complained that in more conservative parts of the US, bookstores were uncomfortable stocking it. A fig leaf would help sales.

When it comes to great art, I don't like fig leafs. But I proposed, just for fun, that we put a peelable fig leaf on the cover so readers could choose whether they wanted their book with or without nudity. My publisher said that would be too expensive. I offered to pay half the cost (10 cents a book times 10,000). He went for it, and I had the fun experience of writing "for fig leafs" on a $500 check. Perhaps that needless expense just bolstered my wish that Americans were more European in their comfort level with nakedness.

The last time I was at a spa in Germany's Black Forest, in one two-hour stretch, I saw more penises than I'd seen in the previous two years. All extremely relaxed...and, I must say, I was struck by the variety. Getting Americans comfortable in the spas with naked Europeans has long been a

The German Spa

When I'm traveling, there are delightful road bumps in my intense research schedule where I put away the notes and simply enjoy the moment. The classic Friedrichsbad spa in Baden-Baden is one of those fine little breaks.

Ever since the Roman Emperor Caracalla soaked in the mineral waters of Baden-Baden, that German spa town has welcomed those in need of a good soak. And it's always naked. In the 19th century, this was Germany's ultimate spa resort, and even today the name Baden-Baden is synonymous with relaxation in a land where the government still pays its overworked citizens to take a little spa time.

I happened to be here when one of our tour groups was in town. I told the guide (who was a German) that I was excited for this great opportunity for her group to enjoy the spa. She disagreed, saying, "No one's going. They can't handle the nudity. That's how it is with American visitors."

They didn't know what they were missing. Wearing only the locker key strapped around my wrist, I began the ritual. I weighed myself: 92 kilos. The attendant led me under the industrial-strength shower, a torrential kickoff pounding my head and shoulders... obliterating the rest of the world. She then gave me slippers and a towel, ushering me into a dry heat room with fine wooden reclining chairs— their slats too hot without the towel. Staring up at exotic tiles of herons and palms, I cooked. After more hot rooms punctuated with showers came the massage.

Like someone really drunk going for one more glass, I climbed gingerly onto the marble slab and lay belly-up. The masseur held up two Brillo-pad mitts and asked, "Hard or soft?" In the spirit of wild abandon, I said, "Hard," not certain what that would mean to my skin. I got the coarse Brillo-pad scrub-down.

I was so soaped up, he had to hold my arms like a fisherman holds a salmon so I wouldn't slip away. With the tenderness of someone gutting a big fish, he scrubbed, chopped, bent, and generally tenderized me. In

challenge and a frustration for me as a guide. I care because, once people get used to it, I find they consider it a great experience. My first European spa visit was with my wife and some German friends—a classy, good-looking young couple. We were swept into the changing area with no explanation, and suddenly the Germans were naked. Eventually we realized everyone was just there to relax. We eased up and got more comfortably naked. It's not sexual...simply open and free.

Whether in a German spa, a Finnish sauna, a Croatian beach, or a Turkish hammam (I can't come up with an English example), a fun part of travel can be getting naked with strangers. Of course, when producing public television, we can't easily show spas, saunas, or beaches in Europe where

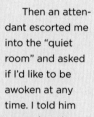

spite of the rough treatment, it was extremely relaxing.

Finished with a Teutonic spank on the butt, I was sent off into the pools. Nude, without my glasses, and not speaking the language, I was gawky. On a sliding scale between Mr. Magoo and Woody Allen, I was everywhere. Steam rooms, cold plunges...it all led to the mixed section.

This is where the Americans get really uptight. The parallel spa facilities intersect, as both men and women share the finest three pools. Here, all are welcome to glide under exquisite domes in perfect silence like aristocratic swans. Germans are nonchalant, tuned into their bodies and focused on solitary relaxation. Tourists are tentative, trying to be cool...but more aware of their nudity.

The climax is the cold plunge. I'm not good with cold water—yet I absolutely love this. You must not wimp out on the cold plunge.

Then an attendant escorted me into the "quiet room" and asked if I'd like to be awoken at any time. I told him at closing time. He wrapped me in hot sheets and a brown blanket. No, I wasn't wrapped...I was swaddled. Warm, flat on my back, among twenty hospital-type beds—only one other bed was occupied...he seemed dead. I stared up at the ceiling, and some time later was jolted awake by my own snore.

Leaving, I weighed myself again: 91 kilos. I had shed 2.2 pounds of sweat. It would have been more if tension had mass. Stepping into the cool evening air, I was thankful my hotel was a level two-block stroll away. Like Gumby, flush and without momentum, I fell slow-motion onto my down comforter, my head buried in a big, welcoming pillow. Wonderfully naked under my clothes, I could only think, "Ahhhh. Baden-Baden."

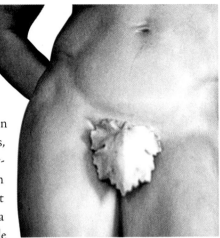

nudity is the norm. Because of strict FCC regulations on nudity, we have to even be careful of which art we show. Because I show art featuring naked bodies, my shows are flagged by the network and, in some more conservative markets, programmers play it safe by airing my shows after 10 p.m., when things are less restrictive. In recent years, programmers actually got a list of how many seconds of marble penis and canvas breast were showing in each episode. They couldn't inflict a Titian painting or a Bernini statue on their viewership in those more conservative communities without taking heat.

Compared to Europe, America has long been laughable in its modesty. Only American tourists are biking into trees as they explore Europe's city parks, which are littered with topless sunbathers. But things got serious during the last decade (with naughty Howard Stern; Bono, soldiers, and football players swearing on TV; and Janet Jackson's notorious "wardrobe malfunction" all pushing the envelope).

"Decency proponents" complained that fines imposed by the FCC for these transgressions had been inconsequential. So, in 2004, Congress approved a tenfold increase, raising fines from $27,000 per incident to $275,000 (with many conservative Members of Congress pushing for even higher fines). Any station airing anything potentially offensive (between all the ads for erectile dysfunction medications) on the public airwaves can be made to pay dearly if some of its viewers complain.

The issue of classical art on TV—a nude *David*, for instance—seems okay for now. But these days, the power of America's moral guard should not be underestimated—especially with politicians from conservative regions quick to do what they can to "shore up" their moralistic base. This has a chilling effect: To be safe, producers are more likely to avoid ideas, words, or images that some Americans could find offensive.

As public broadcasting stations lack the resources to survive a major fine, they are particularly careful in this regard. Many of us who produce broadcast material on a shoestring (like me and public broadcasting in general) have to ponder: Should we put a digital fig leaf on *David's* full-frontal nudity? Bleep Bocaccio's bawdy language? Can I film *The Three Graces* only from the waist up? Will Raphael's randy cupids be labeled "child pornography" and Bernini's *Rape of Persephone* as "S & M"? For now, my partners in public television and I will proceed gingerly—not sure if we can show Venus's breasts. Can we risk the possibility of a $275,000 fine…and is that per nipple?

You may not want to bring the more casual European approach to sex and the human body back home with you. And I'm not saying we should all run around naked. But I suspect that children raised in America, where sex is often considered "dirty," are more likely to have an uncomfortable relationship with sex and their bodies than Europeans do. (I sense that there is more violence associated with sex here than there; in fact, Americans report at least double the incidence of rape as citizens of any European country.) And I have a hunch that the French, who have as many words for a kiss as Eskimos have for snow, enjoy making love more than we Americans do. I like a continent where sexual misconduct won't doom a politician with anyone other than his family and friends, and where the human body is considered a divine work of art worth admiring openly.

Reviving the "Brand of America"

We've covered a lot of ground about how America perceives Europe. Now let's flip things around, to see how Europe perceives America. Sadly, this changed dramatically in the first decade of the 21st century.

OK, I'll admit it: Like two-thirds of Americans—and virtually the entire rest of the planet—I was no fan of George W. Bush. While my differences with him on various philosophical and policy points were matters of personal political opinion, there's no question that the Bush Administration's actions severely blemished the "Brand of America"—how the US is perceived overseas. People in Europe like Americans as much now as they ever did. But there's no doubt that,

throughout the Bush years, their view of the United States as a political entity took a hit.

Americans—mindful of the now-dated "Ugly American" stereotype— tend to be conscientious ambassadors of their country when traveling to Europe. And, particularly because of the Iraq War—even in the post-Bush era—many are fearful that they might receive a negative welcome, especially in France (where anti-war sentiment seemed the most vociferous). Through my tour business, I take a thousand Americans to France annually. Each year, I survey them in an email, asking, "How were you respected by the local people?" Even in the most "anti-American" times, nobody complained. The French have always given American individuals a warm welcome. They just don't always like our foreign policy. In Europe, the mark of a friend is not someone who constantly fawns over your obvious strengths, but someone who tells you when you are off-base and disappointing them.

When European countries refuse to support US foreign policy, many Americans say, "Don't they remember how we saved them from the Nazis?" The answer is yes, absolutely they do. I was recently filming in France's Burgundy, at a charming little mom-and-pop château. When I'm filming, get out of my way—the sun's going down, and we've got work to do. But the aristocratic couple whose family had called that castle home for centuries insisted, "We must stop and have a ceremony because we have an American film crew here working in our castle." They cracked open a fine bottle of wine and brought out—with great ceremony, as if it were a precious relic— the beautiful 48-star American flag they had hoisted over their château on that great day in 1944 when they were freed by the American troops. They implored us, "Please go home and tell your friends that we will never forget what America did for us with its heroics, its economic and military might, and its commitment to liberty." In addition to being grateful to the US for helping to free them from Hitler, Europeans also appreciate our defeat of the Soviet Union with a bold and determined battle of economic attrition during the Cold War.

I have European friends six or eight years older than me, born in the late 1940s, named Frankie and Johnny because their parents were so inspired by the greatness of the Americans they met who came to liberate them from the Nazis. But Europeans no longer name their children after American GIs. The sad reality is that, in the first decade of the 21st century, if your job was marketing a product in Europe, one of your responsibilities was to comb any

Europeans are forever thankful for America's role in freeing them from Nazi tyranny.

hint of America out of your promotional material. "California" used to sell in Europe. But in recent years, it's been the kiss of death.

The "Brand of America" changes with the attitude of whichever administration is setting the tone. With each new president, other nations wonder if there will be unilateralism or multilateralism, respect and collaboration or threats and hypocrisy. Travelers have the opportunity to take home a firsthand understanding of what the rest of the world thinks when it sees America. And if they don't like what they learn, they can work in their own communities to help repair that image problem.

We've taken a wide-ranging and (I hope) thought-provoking tour through the Old World. You probably found some of these ideas appealing, and others appalling. Again I'll state the obvious—that Europe doesn't have all the answers. But I wonder if Europe is "out-innovating" us when it comes to finding clever new solutions. When I encourage Americans to take a look at a European approach to a problem that is befuddling us, some critics accuse me of "America-bashing"—"If you love Europe so much, why don't you just move there?" Short answer: I love America more. And because I care about our society, I challenge us to do better. In difficult times, we should be open to considering all the solutions we can.

•‡•‡•‡•‡•‡•‡•

Seeing European Passions Nurtures a Broader Perspective

Part of the fun of travel is learning to respect and celebrate how different people have different passions for different things. A traveler learns that the love of life, liberty, and the pursuit of happiness comes in different colors and knows no borders. And as this photo essay shows, if there's one thing we can learn from Europe, perhaps it's new ways to enjoy life to its fullest.

▲ Like community events in my hometown are uplifting, little festivals contribute to the fabric of every community. In Verona, Italy, teenage cooks teach the little ones how to make ravioli in hopes of keeping that element of Italian culture vibrant. In spite of its modernity, Europe values its traditions. Festivals seem designed to hand these traditions from one generation to the next.

◀ In Beaune, France, the local Chamber of Commerce invests in an exhibit to help people appreciate the wine. Clearly, having a good nose in France is a life skill worth cultivating.

In America, we have freezers in our garages so we can buy in bulk to save both money and needless trips to the supermarket. In contrast, Europeans have small refrigerators. It's not necessarily because they don't have room or money for a big refrigerator. They'd actually rather go to the market in the morning. The market visit is a chance to be out, get the freshest food, connect with people, and stay in touch. While the popularity of supermarkets is growing, Europeans who value the traditional fabric of their societies still willingly pay a little more for their bread for the privilege of knowing the person who baked it.

In Italy, they love their expensive red wine—but they also love their simple, fill-'er-up-at-the-gas-station wine. Italians get their table wine cheap at filling stations like this.

On the streets of Helsinki, seeing masses of people marching, I thought I might be in store for a big demonstration. Then I realized it was an annual festival where all the choirs gather on the steps of the cathedral. They sang a few hymns together, then they broke into small groups and invaded every pub in town. It's the "take choral music to the pubs" festival.

French farmers fatten their geese to enlarge their livers, considerd a delicacy. They force-feed the geese four times a day. Then, when their livers grow from a quarter-pound to two pounds, they slaughter them and eat the fattened liver, or foie gras. The English travel in droves to France's Dordogne region to enjoy this gourmet treat. Animal-rights activists worldwide object to the treatment of the geese, and for a time, foie gras was actually illegal for restaurants to serve in Illinois. But French farmers don't understand all

the fuss. They tell me the tradition started when their ancestors caught geese who had fattened up their own livers to make the migratory trip to Egypt. They found them very tasty and decided to raise them, help them fatten those livers, and spare them that long flight to Egypt. They claim that geese are designed to grow fat livers, and they pride themselves in creating fine living conditions—as the quality of the foie gras depends on the quality of life the geese lead, right up until the day they are slaughtered.

▲ The biggest single room in America is filled with airplanes. The biggest one in Europe (in Holland) is filled with flowers.

▶ The English have an impressive ability to lie on beaches and pretend it's sunny.

◀ This woman just hiked all the way from Paris to the northwest corner of Spain, Santiago de Compostela. For a thousand years, pilgrims have made this trek for reasons I don't understand. I'll never forget seeing the jubilation on the faces as triumphant trekkers of all ages and languages— walking sticks frayed, pant-legs fringed, faces sunburned—paused to savor the sweet moment when they finally reached their goal. I'm not sure why this moved me so. Perhaps it's the timeless power of individual faith. Maybe it's heritage and tradition. Or it might be the notion that people would abandon everything and move mountains for treasured feelings and beliefs that never even occurred to me.

Regardless of your journey, you can put a little pilgrim in your travels and find your own personal jubilation.

Chapter 4
Resurrection in El Salvador

My three trips to Central America—each organized and led by Augsburg College's Center for Global Education—have done much to shape my politics. The first trip, in 1988, took place during El Salvador's Civil War. By my second visit, in 1991, the leftist people's revolution had been put down and US- and corporate-friendly forces were in control. The third trip, in 2005, was built around the events memorializing the 25th anniversary of the assassination of Archbishop Oscar Romero. (Journals from all of these trips are online at www.ricksteves.com/politicalact.)

For each of these trips, I had a week or two available for a vacation. I could have enjoyed lying on a beach somewhere, but I chose to spend the time in El Salvador. Checking in on a people who lost a revolution, taking the pulse of corporate-led globalization in a poor country, collecting my impressions, and sharing them now is precisely what I consider to be travel as a political act.

I realize it's odd, as a relative novice to Latin American travel, for me to have such strong opinions—or any opinion, for that matter—on these topics. It's clear: My passion is rooted in the opportunities I've had to talk with and learn from smart, poor people living in what I grew up considering "banana republics." Frankly, spending time with the poor in Central America radicalizes people from the rich world. I hope the following impressions and observations—mostly from my 2005 trip—not only share some of what I learned, but illustrate why choosing a place like Managua over a place like Mazatlán the next time you head south of the border can create a more fulfilling travel experience.

Travel Makes You Wiser, but Less Happy

As we prepared to leave Miami, a flight attendant who liked my TV show bumped me from coach to first class. Alone among leather seats with my drink in a real glass, I thought about the congestion—noisy families, people trying to jam all their cheap new electronic gadgets overhead—back in economy. I

This bus tour is filled with Americans eager to learn and hungry for inspiration.

felt more than wealthy. I felt elite. Looking out the window into the Caribbean night, I pondered my privileged position. A chain of lights led to Key West. Then, deep in the blackness, glittered the forbidden city of Havana. The pilot's door was locked and fortified as we flew to El Salvador.

Landing in the capital city, San Salvador, I was met by César, who whisked me away in his car. In his coin dish, I saw shiny Lincolns and Washingtons. I'm never very confident upon arrival in a new country, and this confused me. César explained, "We've been dollarized now since 2001." Since my last visit here, my coins had become the local coins. (In a kind of voluntary colonization, local elites chose to adopt the US currency to avoid losing their personal fortunes in case of a radical change in their government.) My hunch was that much more had changed in El Salvador than just the currency.

Back before my first trip to Central America in 1988, I specifically forbade my heart to get caught up in economic justice issues south of our border. I knew there were leftists fighting American-funded groups and it was a tragic mess, but that was it. There was too much pulling at me, and the competing sides, excuses, and complaints were all too complex and contradictory. I just didn't have the energy to sort it out, and I didn't need it in my life. Then I traveled here and I learned what Thomas Jefferson meant when he wrote that travel "makes men wiser, but less happy."

Where and how you choose to travel determines how much you'll learn. Organizations offering "educational tours" turn the world into a fascinating classroom.

That first trip lit a fire in me. I realized I have the right, if not the responsibility, to form my opinions based on my own experience, even if it goes against the mainstream at home. It was liberating, empowering...and exhausting. After that first trip, I published my journal, flew to Washington, DC, and spent two days hand-delivering it to the office of each Member of Congress on Capitol Hill. Deep down I knew that my efforts would likely end up in congressional recycling bins, but I needed to do it. And doing it felt good. That little mission marked the start of the time when my travels became more than just recreation.

El Salvador politics line up on two sides: The left includes the FMLN guerillas-turned-politicians, students, labor groups, Protestant churches, and many Catholic priests and nuns (especially those who espouse a Liberation Theology approach). The right includes the dominant ARENA party, the military (and Civil War–era death squads), big business, wealthy elites, and the official Catholic Church hierarchy. These two forces are locked in a seemingly endless battle for the souls of El Salvador's *campesinos* (peasants). The US typically supports the right wing, both to protect its own economic interests and—back in the 1980s—to fight the perceived "communist threat" of the left.

While the players remain the same, the game has changed. The peace that ended the country's Civil War also ushered in an era of globalization. By my third visit, in 2005, North American chains—from Pizza Hut to Texaco to Subway—were thriving. The Marlboro Man looked good on his horse. And, as I cruised through town past a cancan of American-owned franchises, it seemed the victory of the US-supported faction had been a huge success.

But living in San Salvador—a city of a million and a half people—was still no picnic. It had been 13 years since the end of the Civil War, five years since the collapse of the coffee industry, and four years since two huge earthquakes devastated the country. El Salvador had the highest homicide rate of any city in the Western Hemisphere, and gang violence was on the rise. Exploring San Salvador, it was clear that any nice home came with a fenced-in and fortified front yard. Rolls of razor wire were on sale in the newspaper for just $33. In the wealthy neighborhoods, each street had an armed guard. Every sizable business also posted a guard.

The relative lack of news about Latin America since the 1980s had lulled me into thinking that perhaps things were getting better for people there. But suffering that's not covered on the nightly news is still suffering. This trip reminded me of the power of our media—even over those of us who are determined not to be misled.

Under a Corrugated Tin Roof with Beatriz

El Salvador provides the *norteamericano* with a hot and muggy welcome. After one day, I had settled in quite well. I was speckled with bug bites and accustomed to my frail cold shower, noisy fan, and springy cot. I knew to brush my teeth with bottled water and to put used toilet paper in the waste basket to avoid clogging the toilet. I was ready for some serious education... and I got it. I was shocked to learn how amazingly blind I was to people's daily reality just a short plane ride south of the border.

Local experts briefed us on the state of El Salvador's economy. The minimum wage was about $1 an hour ($144 a month). While in the US, minimum wage is considered a starting point, most Salvadorans aspire only to minimum wage...and that's all they get.

When coffee prices crashed in the early 2000s, that crop went from providing 50 percent of the country's export earnings to about 3 percent. With legions of coffee workers suddenly unemployed, their children were hopeless and directionless. Many teens were left with little to do but roam the cities in gangs and cause better-off people to build even higher walls. The *maquiladora* industry (sewing clothing for rich world corporations looking for cheap labor) moved in and now makes up 25 percent of the local economy.

To make ends meet, most Salvadoran families struggle to send one person abroad to earn money. Seven in ten families have an immediate member in the US—about two million total. In 2005, remittances (money sent home from these expats) brought $2.5 billion into El Salvador—or 16 percent of the country's entire economy. "Refugee aid" like this is big throughout the developing world. In fact, in 2004, the total amount of money that refugees working in the rich world sent home to their families (an estimated $75 billion) was fifty percent higher than all foreign aid combined ($50 billion).

In 2001, two huge earthquakes killed over a thousand Salvadorans (in a nation of about six million people). They destroyed or badly damaged a quarter of the private homes in the country, leaving 1.5 million homeless. Of course, in a big shake, it's the poor whose homes crumble—seismic safety is a luxury only the privileged can afford. (An earthquake of the same magnitude hit my hometown of Seattle that same year, and no one died.) The best those

living in a shantytown can do for protection is to live in what they call "miniskirt housing"—cinderblocks for the lower half of the walls, and then light corrugated tin for the upper walls and roof. If a miniskirt house tumbles down, it won't kill you. And when it's over, you just scavenge a few two-by-fours, reassemble the frame, and nail your sheets of tin back in place.

The Western Union office is a busy place in El Salvador. Money wired home from immigrant laborers in the US keeps many Central American families afloat.

In the midst of relative affluence, Americans seem to operate with a mindset of scarcity—focusing on what we don't have or what we might lose. Meanwhile, Salvadorans I met, with so little, embrace life with a mindset of abundance—thankful for the simple things they do have.

Our group dropped in on Beatriz and her daughter Veronica, who live in a miniskirt shack on El Salvador's minimum wage. The place was as clean and inviting as a tin-roofed shack with a dirt floor can be. Beatriz sat us down and told of raising a family through a Civil War:

"The war moved into the capital, and our little house happened to sit between the police headquarters and the guerillas. At night I hid with my children under the bed as bullets flew. For ten years, the war put us in never-ending fear. Mothers feared the forced recruitment of our sons. Finally, we arranged a peace. But the peace accords didn't benefit us poor people." She explained how this "peace" was no more than an acknowledgement of the futility of a continued struggle. To this day people are unhappy. In some regions, there is even talk about taking up arms once more. Beatriz said, "If war started again, I think some of us would die from the stress."

About her life, she said, "My house becomes a lake in the rainy season. Still, we are thankful to have this place. Our land was very cheap. We bought it from a man receiving death threats. He fled to America. While we make $144 a month in the city, the minimum out in the countryside is much less—only $70 a month. Nearly half the families in our country are living on $1 a day per person. To survive, you need a home that is already in your family. You have one light bulb, corn, and beans. That is about all. Living on minimum wage is more difficult now than before the war. Before, electricity cost about $1 a month. Water was provided. Today electricity costs $19 and water $14—that's about one-quarter of my monthly wage. My mother has a tumor in her head. There is no help possible. I have no money."

Beatriz's 22-year-old daughter, Veronica, was as strikingly beautiful as one of the Latina stars so hot on the popular scene. She dreamed of going to the US, but the "coyote" (as the guy who ferries refugees across Mexico and into the US is called) would charge $6,000, and she would probably be raped before reaching the US border as a kind of "extra fee."

As a chicken with a bald neck pecked at my shoe, I surveyed the ingenious mix of mud, battered lumber, and corrugated tin that made up this house. It occurred to me that poverty erodes ethnic distinctions. There's something uniform about desperation.

Beatriz and Veronica prepared for us their basic meal: a corn tortilla. As I ate a thick corn cake hot off the griddle, it felt like I was taking communion. In that tortilla were tales of peasants who bundled their tortillas into a bandana and ran through the night as American helicopters swept across their skies.

For me, munching on that tortilla provided a sense of solidarity—wimpy...but still solidarity. I was what locals jokingly call a "round-trip revolutionary" (someone from a stable and wealthy country who cares enough to come down here...but only with a return plane ticket in hand). Still, having had the opportunity to sit and talk with Beatriz and Veronica, even a round-trip revolutionary flies home with an indelible understanding of the human reality of that much-quoted statistic, "Half of humanity is trying to live on $2 a day."

Globalization: The -Ism of Our Time

Beatriz and Veronica—and you and I—are players in a vast global chess game of commerce. As the world's economy evolves, modern technology is shrinking the planet, putting the labor, natural resources, and capital of distant lands in touch with each other and revolutionizing the way products are made and marketed. Globalization is a complicated process that, frankly, nobody can control or even fully understand. But the people I met in El Salvador made it more meaningful for me than any book or lecture ever could. Free trade, neoliberalism, and globalization—which are abstract political buzzwords back home—are all too real to the half of humanity struggling for survival.

The rich world likes to imagine that globalization brings needed resources to poor nations. And often, it does. In this equation, a company from a wealthy country decides to have their product manufactured in a poor country. The company enjoys a much lower payroll than if they employed workers back home, while still paying a wage that's considered generous in the local economy. It's a win-win. At least, that's the hope.

But in reality, all too often, globalization is driven not by altruism, but by a naked ambition to open new markets to firms and products. The legally mandated responsibility of a corporation is to maximize profits. (Technically, to do anything less opens its officers up to lawsuits from stockholders.) If the only way to do so is to exploit cheap labor in poor countries, they do it. That's why, if you talk with people in El Salvador, even proponents of globalization don't claim anything compassionate about it. It's presented simply as unstoppable: "Globalization is a big train, and it's moving out. Get on or get run over."

I believe we Americans have a moral responsibility to implement globalization conscientiously. I worry that, since the end of the Cold War, the US has been pushing globalization with an almost religious zeal. Our ideological

export after the defeat of communism is free trade. The World Bank, International Monetary Fund (IMF), and World Trade Organization (WTO) are our crusaders. Americans are rightly proud to champion freedom and liberty. But traveling in Latin America, I heard leftist leaders offer a different interpretation: "Sure, freedom for the USA to take other people's natural resources, and liberty to use their cheap labor."

Why so cynical? When globalization was taking root in the early 1990s in places like El Salvador, their US-friendly governments chose growth over policies designed to protect labor and the environment. Still today, if a country has a sick economy, the medicine is predictable: "structural adjustment." That means new laws that protect investors from governments who may someday want to defend their people from the will of aggressive corporations. The end result: Corporations become stronger than the governments of the nations who host them...and the needs of those corporations begin to trump the needs of the nation's own citizens.

In Central America, egregious examples of mishandled globalization are numerous. In the aftermath of their devastating 2001 earthquakes, Salvadorans saw American capitalists roll up their sleeves and speed to the rescue. Clothing manufacturers moved into the earthquake-devastated area to provide jobs...on the condition that the government allow them to lower the minimum wage from $144 a month to $85 a month.

Folk remedies are the salvation of poor *campesinos* who can't afford the drugs sold by pharmaceutical companies. But the people of neighboring Honduras were recently forced to sell patent rights for these local plants to the

Globalization, Cultural Fragmentation, and Terrorism

Globalization is all about bigger units—economic consolidation. More and more banks, publishers, and airlines survive only by consolidating. Family farms can't compete and are plowed under by big agriculture. And many national economies will thrive only if they also consolidate. In an age when many international corporations have a greater reach and power than entire countries (ExxonMobil has the same economy as Austria—$370 billion; Toyota has the same economy as Venezuela—$230 billion), nations are joining together in ever-bigger free trade zones. A primary goal driving the unification of Europe, for instance, was the creation of that vast free trade zone.

As globalization shrinks our planet, people worry that their rights, livelihoods, and identities—religious, national, and cultural—are in jeopardy.

This means that as our world consolidates economically, it ignites forces that can divide it culturally. As groups perceive that their values and ways of life are threatened, they will embrace even more strongly their cultural distinctions. This is already happening, and issues of cultural and national pride are becoming politicized: Americans fly the Stars and Stripes from car antennas, while Muslim immigrants riot over a cartoon that insults their prophet and insist their children be allowed to wear their headscarves in public schools. This creates a fearful, schizophrenic dynamic that may stoke today's terrorism and tomorrow's international conflicts. As this fear and nationalism make peaceful coexistence more challenging, the value of people building understanding through travel will be greater than ever.

From Texas to Thailand, globalization and its resulting consolidation threaten cultural traditions as well as family farms.

American biotech giant Monsanto...which now has the legal right to charge rural Hondurans for using their own traditional remedies.

Trade levies, which increase with processing, make it easy for a poor country to export raw peanuts. But the prohibitively higher tariff for *processed* peanuts makes it nearly impossible to produce peanut butter competitively outside of the already developed world. (While the most widely used term for poor countries is "developing world," I find that label ironic—since economic policies like this one systematically keep these places *under*developed.)

Many participants like to think of globalization as "tough love," as the rich world tries to pull up the poor world. The scorecard tells a different story. In the last 40 years, the average annual income in the world's 20 poorest countries—places where people make on average less than $1,000 a year— has barely changed. In that same period, the average per capita income in the richest 20 nations has nearly tripled to over $30,000. The bottom 50 percent of humanity lives on roughly 5 percent of the planet's resources. The top 20 percent lives on over 80 percent. The greatest concentration of wealth among economic elites in the history of the human race is happening at the same time our world is becoming a global village.

So what am I? Anti-globalization? No. I'm just anti–*bad* globalization. I do my best not to fall into a knee-jerk "*campesinos* good, corporations bad" school of thinking. I believe that the rich don't necessarily get rich at the expense of the poor. (As conservatives like to say, "It's not a zero-sum game.") If implemented thoughtfully and compassionately, globalization could be the salvation of the developing world. Progress can include or exclude the poor. And, as wealthy people who reap the benefits of globalization, we have an obligation to be responsible.

As a businessman who manufactures some of my travel bags in South Asia, I'm keenly aware that globalization can be either a force for good or a force for harm. I have struggled with and understand the inevitability and moral challenge of it—there's simply no way to produce a bag that will sell without finding the least expensive combination of quality, labor, and materials. I contribute to globalization only because I'm confident that the people who stitch and sew my bags are treated well and paid appropriately. They work for a fraction of the cost of an American, they appreciate the employment, and American consumers want the cheap prices. If I believed that the factory conditions were bad for that community or for its workers, I'd take my business elsewhere. To ensure this, I fly one of my staff to the factory for a periodic re-evaluation. It's a carefully weighed decision that I make with my humanitarian principles (and with the plight of Beatriz and Veronica) in mind.

Even if the rudiments of globalization didn't make people's eyes glaze over, it's human nature not to want to know how our affluence impacts others. No comfortable American enjoys being told how her cat has more "buying power" than some hungry child just south of the border, how his investments may be contributing to the destruction of the environment, how the weaponry we sell and profit from is really being used, or how—if you really knew its story—there's blood on your banana. Privilege brings with it the luxurious option of obliviousness. Most Americans don't understand or particularly care about the impact of a new IMF regulation on a person who sews clothing in Honduras or plants coffee beans in Nicaragua. Here in the rich world, the choice is ours: awareness and concern, or ignorance and bliss.

The City Built Upon a Garbage Dump

San Salvador's poorest neighborhood—a place that makes Beatriz's neighborhood seem almost posh—is built upon a garbage dump. We wandered for an hour around this "city" of 50,000 inhabitants, dusty frills of garbage blowing like old dandelion spores in the wind.

It was a ramshackle world of corrugated tin, broken concrete, and tattered laundry. I'll not forget the piles of scrap metal, the ripped and shredded sofas, tire parts, and filthy plastic bowls I saw stacked neatly at one point. This was a store entirely stocked by junk scavenged from the city dump. Even the store's chairs, tables, walls, and roof were scavenged—made of battered tin.

Overlooking the shacks was a slap-in-your-face billboard from a local bank, advertising home loans for the wealthy. It read, "With every day that passes, your house is closer to being yours."

We passed through a "suburb" of tin shacks housing people who lived off the dump, passing yards where they sorted out saleable garbage, stacked broken glass, and pounded rusty metal barrels into cooking pots and pans. In a church there was a sandbox manger scene with two soldiers standing over a slashed and bloody *campesino* positioned next to the Wise Men and cows—the modern-day soldiers represented the government, while the poor people saw themselves as Christ figures, crucified for the truth.

The people had done what they could to make their slum livable. There was greenery, cute children bringing home huge jugs of water (two cents each),

In my travels—whether to El Salvador, Europe, or Iran—I find that many people outside our borders think of the US as an "empire." But anytime I mention this back home, I get a feisty response. (Don't shoot me. I'm just the jester.)

Americans hate thinking of themselves as an empire. After all, weren't we fighting an "empire" in our Revolutionary War? And wasn't it an "empire" that crucified Jesus and persecuted his followers? The USA—that bastion of freedom and democracy—might not literally claim other countries as part of our own territory. But only we can declare someone else's natural resources on the far side of our planet "vital to our national security" (but which, in reality, are vital only to maintaining our accustomed material lifestyle).

You could debate long and hard about whether the US is an "empire." But actually, what you and I think is irrelevant. The fact is, much of the world *views* us that way, and therefore they—especially our enemies—will treat us as an empire.

Why are we perceived as an empire by so many people? For starters, look at our United Nations voting record: According to the UN website, in 2007, the US voted "no" more than any other nation. In 40 percent of those "no" votes, we were outvoted by at least 150 to 4. Who stands with us as we oppose issues such as creating a declaration of rights for indigenous peoples, the human right to food, child labor laws, dropping the embargo against Cuba, and restricting illicit small arms trade? Israel, Marshall Islands, and Micronesia. Even if you write off the United Nations as a group of one-world-fixated loonies, many other countries take it seriously...and our dismissal of it speaks volumes about our willingness to engage in peaceful and constructive problem-solving.

When others look at us, rather than see a hardworking policeman of the world defending freedom wherever we can, they see a nation with military bases in 130 countries. They see a nation with 4 percent of this planet's people spending as much on their military as everybody else put together.

Some might brush off questionable American policies by saying, "Well, that was just our government." *We* are our government. We cannot rest on the notion of the "innocent civilian." Morally, when it comes to a free and powerful nation like ours, I believe there are no innocent civilians. If I pay taxes, I am a combatant. Every bullet that flies and every bomb that drops has my name on it. It could be a good bomb or a good bullet. Sometimes military action is necessary. But right or wrong, I take moral responsibility for it. That's simply honest, responsible citizenship.

Many Americans consider the emblems of the Bush years—Iraq War, Guantánamo, the Abu Ghraib torture scandal, world isolation, domestic surveillance, loss of civil liberties, and so on—a reasonable price to pay because we avoided another terrorist attack. Much of the rest of the world saw these as an overreaction to a tragic situation. The wave of sympathy that poured into America after 9/11 could have lifted the whole world to an unprecedented new unity. Instead, our leaders manipulated our national grief

to justify acts that have alienated us from many of our allies and swollen the ranks of our enemies.

Every empire in history has been plagued by angry forces on its fringes that refused to play by the rules. Romans were pestered and ultimately defeated by barbarians. The British dealt with and lost to colonial American guerilla patriots. The Habsburgs were plagued by what they derided as "anarchists"...and were eventually defeated. And today, if you're hugely outgunned—as all enemies of America are—you get creative. You shoot from the bushes like we did when we fought the Redcoats. Sure, we might like our enemies to follow our rules...to line up in formation so we can carpet-bomb them. But our enemies know that if someone decides to fight the US, they have two choices; be dead, or be "a terrorist."

In our generation, America risks going broke and selling its soul to fight its "War on Terror." The problem is that there's always been terrorism and there always will be terrorism. It's a technique, not an enemy. And because the targeted "enemy" is a technique, you can fight a "War on Terror"...but you cannot win it.

On a recent visit to Washington, DC, I heard lawmakers using the terms "hard power" and "soft power." Hard power assumes that military might is the best way to get what you want. Soft power respects the influence of something less tangible: goodwill. Winning the "hearts and minds" of our would-be enemies, and improving the so-called "Brand of America," makes it harder for foreign terrorists or bombastic leaders to mobilize people against us. Imagine a US president presenting himself in a way that makes it impossible for the leader of a country we're at odds with to demonize America in order to stay in power. Imagine using our military to build bridges and highways instead of blowing them up. It'd be better for the innocent people who live in those places (not to mention better for our troops). While this might seem a little too "touchy-feely" for our militaristic society, it's less expensive—and certainly less destructive—than hard power.

If we can soften the way we wield our power, we might find some solutions that work better for us...and for the rest of the planet. Is this naive? Maybe. But as we've seen, it's clear the opposite approach has its flaws, too.

Even when people around the world are frustrated by our policies, they're still inspired by the ideals of America. And, after nearly four decades of travels through political ups and downs—even when I talk with Salvadorans whose families were torn apart by US-funded soldiers—it's clear to me that people across the world want to like Americans. My travels have taught me that we have friends everywhere ready to put the past behind them and to once again be inspired by both our ideals and our leadership.

and lots of mud, bamboo, and corrugated tin buildings. As we approached the ridge overlooking the main dump, I started thinking that this really wasn't all that awful.

Then we entered a kind of living hell. We'd heard of the people living off garbage dumps, and now we were in for a firsthand look: huge bulldozers, circling black birds, and a literal mountain of garbage ten stories high with people picking through it. It was a vast urban fruit rind covered with human flies.

A policeman with a machine gun kept the people away from one half of the garbage mountain. That was where aid items that the government figured would cost them too much to disperse were being buried under the garbage. About thirty people gathered. Our guide said they were waiting for the guard to leave. I couldn't believe him. Then the guard left, and all thirty scavengers broke into a run and dashed into the best part of the dump. The smell was sweet and sickening.

Overwhelmed by the uncomfortable realities I was confronted with, I retreated to a strip mall in a wealthy part of town. I was just settling into a nice, peaceful, comforting latte, like I get each morning back home, when a US military helicopter surged over the horizon. It hovered above for a moment and then clumsily landed. A jolly Santa Claus hopped out to the delight of the children wealthy enough to have moms shopping here.

Looking at those kids and thinking of their dump-dwelling cousins, I realized that, even if you're motivated only by greed, if you know what's good for you, you don't want to be filthy rich in a desperately poor world. I've seen it here in Central America, where the wealthy

Painted clay figurines featuring a bloody, slain peasant (the "Christ figure") at the feet of two camouflaged, US-equipped-and-funded soldiers (considered "the new centurions," tools of empire) filled Central American Christmas markets during my visit. During the heat of the Civil War, poor Salvadoran children scooted these gory trios into their manger scenes along with Mary, Joseph, and the shepherds. They are a vivid Liberation Theology reminder of Roman Empire/American Empire parallels and how Christ knows their struggles. I keep this statue—my favorite souvenir from that trip—on a prominent shelf in my office.

Older kids watch younger kids while dads scavenge and moms walk for water.

have speed bumps in front of their fancy houses, forcing angry bomb-throwers to slow down long enough for guards to get their license-plate number. I've seen it in Java, hanging out with rich Chinese behind designer fortifications. And I've seen it in Dallas, driving out to Plano past ten miles of fortified front yards with chicken wire over the top to protect relatively wealthy children from the have-nots who roam those fine streets.

Feeling the breeze of the chopper as Santa climbed back in and it flew away, I took another sip of the drink I just paid half a day's local wages for. Pulling out my little notebook, I added a few more observations, and continued my education.

In 1492, Columbus Sailed the Ocean Blue...

Our Salvadoran hosts gave us a history lesson unlike any I got in my schooling. In 1524, the Spaniards arrived in El Salvador. They killed people, burned villages, and named the place "The Savior" after Christ. Enslaving the locals—branding them with hot irons like cattle—those first conquistadors established a persistent pattern.

Under the Spanish, land long used to grow corn (the local staple) was re-cultivated to grow indigo (a better cash crop for export). As indigo needed flat land, locals were displaced and pushed into the hills. Later, when the rise of cotton wiped out the indigo trade, coffee became El Salvador's top cash crop. Coffee needed to be grown on the hillside. So the people were displaced again.

Rebellion after rebellion was put down as the land was Christianized. Making religion the opiate of the masses, the priests preached, "Don't question authority. Heaven awaits those who suffer quietly." (Even today, when labor organizers try to mobilize workers against structural poverty, they hear, "No, our struggles are God's will." Those promoting the left-wing people's party report that their

challenge is to teach poor Christian peasants that it's okay to get political and vote for change.)

El Salvador won its independence from Spain in 1821. The local victors were not the indigenous people, but the descendants of those first Spanish conquistadors. They wanted to continue harvesting El Salvador...but without giving Spain its

While political murals are dangerous these days, indigenous Salvadorans—who call themselves "people of corn"—celebrate their ethnicity instead.

cut. Indigenous Salvadorans gained nothing from "independence."

After the popular uprisings and massacres of 1932, indigenous culture was outlawed, the left wing was decimated, and a military dictatorship was established. Those who spoke the indigenous language were killed. Traditional dress was prohibited. After 1932, when a white person looked at an Indian, the Indian's head would drop. To be indigenous was to be subversive. And today, the word *indígena* still comes with negative connotations: illiterate, ignorant, savage.

In the Bible, God calls for a Jubilee Year (Leviticus 25:10)—every fifty years, the land is to be redistributed and debts are to be forgiven. Perhaps God figured that, given the greedy nature of humankind, it takes about fifty years for economic injustice to build to a point that drives a society to violence.

Rich Christians can't imagine God was serious. But the sad modern history of El Salvador shows the wisdom in the Biblical Jubilee year. There's a pattern that I think of as Jubilee massacres: a dramatic spike in violence every fifty years. Twice a century, landless peasants rise up...and are crushed. In the 1830s, an insurrection and its charismatic leader were put down. In 1881, peasants suffered a big and bloody land grab. In 1932, after the great global depression and communist influence made landless peasants both hungry and bold, an estimated 30,000 were massacred following an insurrection. In the 1980s, the people rose up and were repressed so cruelly that a 12-year civil war followed. The 1830s, 1881, 1932, the 1980s—during the last two centuries, El Salvador has endured a slaughter every fifty years.

A monument much like America's Vietnam Veterans Memorial stands in San Salvador, remembering people killed in its most recent popular uprising.

Thoughtful travelers who respect the Bible can make a point to read it as the majority of Christians on this planet do: through the eyes of the poor world. Christians with two different outlooks could read Matthew 25, where Christ says, "I was hungry and you fed me, imprisoned and you visited me, naked and you clothed me. What you have done to the least of people, you have done to me." One could be motivated to find ways to tackle structural poverty in poor nations. The other might think that's naive, and continue pounding plowshares into swords.

El Salvador's Civil War and Bonsai Democracy
There's a popular saying in the poor world: Feed the hungry and you're a saint. Ask why they are hungry and you are a communist. In the 1970s, Central American priests started asking why. These Liberation Theologians threatened the powerful...and were killed.

When Oscar Romero was made archbishop in 1977, wealthy Salvadorans breathed a sigh of relief. If his reputation as a fairly conservative priest was any indication of how he would run the Church here, they believed the right wing had nothing to fear. But the growing violence against the poor and the assassinations of church leaders who grappled with economic injustice drove Romero to speak out. Eventually this mild-mannered priest became the charismatic spokesperson of his people.

As a Liberation Theologian, Romero invited his followers to see Christmas as the story of a poor, homeless mother with a hungry baby. Romero taught that the lessons and inspiration offered by the Bible were tools for the faithful as they dealt with the struggles of their day-to-day lives.

Because Archbishop Oscar Romero asked why, he was gunned down in 1980 in front of his congregation. Then, dozens of worshippers were murdered at his funeral.

After the killing of Romero, the poor—emboldened by their Liberation Theology—rebelled, plunging El Salvador into their long and bloody Civil War. The united guerilla front (FMLN) expected a quick win, but the US under President Reagan spent $1.5 million a day to keep that from happening. With the success of the Sandinistas in Nicaragua in July 1979, Reagan was determined to stop the spread of what he considered a communist threat.

El Salvador's Archbishop Oscar Romero.

Salvadoran forces assumed, because the guerillas were maintaining their strength, that innocent civilians in leftist-controlled territory were no longer innocent. Civilian women and children were considered combatants— fair game—in order for the popular revolt to become less popular. As if draining the sea to kill the fish, right-wing forces targeted and terrorized civilians with a brutal vengeance. Notorious "death squads" wrought havoc on El Salvador's poor. Today this policy, considered an option for quelling insurgencies around the world, is known as the "Salvador Option."

While the FMLN could have fought on, the toll on their country was too great. In 1984, negotiations began that finally led to a 1992 peace accord. The negotiated settlement ending the Civil War meant the guerilla forces would trade in their guns for a spot in the government. Suddenly, the guerillas shaved, washed, and found themselves members of parliament representing a now-peaceful FMLN party.

Today, the FMLN is a legitimate political force in El Salvador. Rather than the more sinister black and red of its guerilla rebellion days, FMLN propaganda comes in a cheerier white and red. They are welcome…as long as they don't get too powerful. Democracy in countries that function as the quarries of capitalism reminds

When asked "Who really runs El Salvador?," most Salvadorans would say simply, "The Embassy" (as the American Embassy is called here). You can't miss it: It's just above San Salvador, built upon the ruins of the old pre-Columbian Indian capital.

me of a bonsai tree: You keep it in the window for others to see, and when it grows too big, you cut it back.

Who does the cutting? It's still the USA. Much as US corporations wield an undue influence over Latin American business, the US government continues to exert its authority over "democracies" south of our border. For example, in El Salvador's 2004 presidential elections, the left-wing FMLN candidate seemed poised to win. The US sent an envoy, Jeb Bush, to El Salvador to feed the rumor that if the FMLN won, the US would expel the two million Salvadorans living in America. The loss of money from these Salvadoran expats sent to their starving relatives back home would be devastating. A TV ad showed a woman opening an envelope from the US and reading a letter from her son: "Sorry, mom, if the FMLN wins, this will be the last money I can send from the USA." A week later, the right wing and US-friendly ARENA party won big.

You can argue whether American meddling in Latin American politics is justified. Either way, it makes me uncomfortable to think that a nation founded on the principles of liberty and freedom wields such a strong influence over fledgling democracies. In recent decades, throughout the developing world, the US has made it clear that if the left-wing candidates win, "relations will suffer."

I asked Father Jon Sobrino (a leading Jesuit priest and scholar at the University of Central America) about America's influence on Salvadoran politics. He said, "These days, when I hear the word 'democracy,' my bowels move."

Liberation Theology

If economic elites use religion as the "opiate of the masses," Liberation Theology is the opposite. Liberation Theology is a politicized view of Christianity popular among the world's poor and those trying to inspire the poor to fight for economic justice. Liberation theologians preach that every person is created in God's image, and God intended them to have dignity. They say economic injustice and structural poverty are an affront to God, and it is right for the downtrodden to mobilize and fight for their God-given rights now rather than docilely wait for heavenly rewards.

Liberation Theology has easy-to-trace roots. In 1959, the success of the Cuban Revolution inspired revolutionary movements throughout Central America. In 1965, Vatican II encouraged the faithful to take their religion a little more personally. In 1968, the Catholic bishops of Latin America met at Medellín (in Colombia). They called for Christians to live out the gospel and encouraged them to find dignity while on earth. Although it didn't have a name yet, this was Liberation Theology.

The movement was officially born in 1972, when Gustavo Gutiérrez published *A Theology of Liberation*. The 1970s saw the rise of the first Christian Base Communities, which incorporated this take on Christianity into their daily lives. In these Liberation Theology-driven barrios, resurrection is the responsibility of the community. When one is killed, he or she lives on in the community.

As it was in feudal Europe, the power centers in Central America have been the military, the landowners, and the Church. After Vatican II and the bishops' conference at Medellín, the Church decided to embrace Jesus' "preferential option" (or special concern) for the poor. When this happened, the old alliance (state, church, and land-owning elites)—which had so effectively kept the people down—began breaking apart. Revolution followed.

Liberation Theology was serious stuff, and the US took note. President Nixon dispatched future Vice President Nelson Rockefeller to Latin America to find out exactly what it was. He helped establish an American Cold War stance that considered this politicization of Christianity (with its Marxist underpinnings) a direct challenge to American interests in Central America.

From this point on, the story of El Salvador's struggle became a story of martyrs. First, politically active peasants were killed. From the 1970s on, Church leaders were targeted. "Be a patriot...kill a priest" was a bumper sticker-like slogan popular among El Salvador's national guard.

The 1980s was the golden age of Liberation Theology. But, while it gave hope to millions of previously hopeless people, the movement also had many critics. Mingling religious authority with social, political, and even military power, Liberation Theology could lead to armed revolution. And it had a potentially corrupting influence on local charismatic priests, who created a cult of personality to empower themselves and their followers. Still, lacking an equally uplifting alternative, many people see Liberation Theology as the only viable option for people dissatisfied with what they consider

Many "escape theology" rallies in places like El Salvador are funded by like-minded Christians in the US. The sermon here would promote these principles: Heaven and earth are separate. Wealth is a blessing, and poverty is God's will. Be obedient to authority, both church and political. Accepting your place in life is a key to your salvation. When you die, you'll be rewarded in heaven.

a social and economic structure that keeps them poor.

In the 1990s, after the peace accords ended the Civil War, this revolutionary movement morphed into a political party (FMLN), and the Christian Base Communities slowly lost their vibrancy. Today, Liberation Theology seems dormant as a political force. The progressive side of the Catholic Church has been tamed.

Instead, there's been a resurgence of "escape theology"—the apolitical yin to Liberation Theology's yang—in the form of fundamentalism. North American televangelists supplement this empire-friendly approach to Christianity by inspiring their followers to send money so the downtrodden south of our border can be taught to "just say no" when it comes to the political struggle for dignity. The charismatic, US-friendly Pentecostal faith—with an emphasis on building a personal relationship with Christ, rather than dealing with the root causes of economic injustice—is also booming. This "suffer now, enjoy later" theology keeps the opiate in religion. These days, in many El Salvador churches, it's taboo to talk politics. When it comes to economic injustice, don't ask why.

Traveling—whether in Christian, Muslim, Hindu, or Buddhist lands—you see how religion injects passion into local politics. Lessons learned on the road tend to give me both empathy for people's struggles and a respect for the importance of separation of religion and state. Just as I oppose prayer in school in the US, I don't like it when a Muslim society becomes a theocracy and legislates morality according to Quranic values. Yet when a politicized Church (such as the one that stood by the revolutionaries of Central America in the 1980s) fights for economic justice, I find myself rooting for the politicization of religion. My heart makes my politics inconsistent.

Romero, Martyrdom, and Resurrection

The reason for my 2005 visit to El Salvador was to remember Romero on the 25th anniversary of his assassination. Marching with thousands of his followers through the streets of San Salvador, it was clear to me…just as Romero prophesized, they killed him, yet he lives through his people.

I'll never forget the parade that day. Everyone in our group crayoned *Romero Vive* ("Romero lives") on our white T-shirts. We piled into the repainted but obviously recycled circa 1960s American school bus (the standard public transport in Central America today), drove as close as we could, and then spilled into the streets. Joining masses of Salvadorans, we funneled through their capital city and to the cathedral, which held the body of their national hero. Entrepreneurs sold bananas from woven bins and drinks in clear

Americans march with Salvadorans 25 years after the assassination of Romero.

plastic bags pierced by paper straws. Parents packed along children born long after Romero's day. Prune-faced old ladies who couldn't handle the long march filled the backs of beat-up pickup trucks, adding slow-rolling "granny floats" to the parade of people. Banks, Western Union offices, strip malls, and fast-food joints seemed to stand still and observe as the marchers shut down the city. Soldiers looking on appeared humbled by the crowd.

Just being there put me in solidarity with a powerful and surging people's spirit. Being a head taller than anyone else and clearly a *norteamericano*, I had lots of friends. Judging from the smiles I encountered, my presence was appreciated.

The parade culminated at the cathedral where, in his last sermon there, Romero had directed his words to the soldiers: "You are brothers of the poor. These are your people. More important than any order from your commanders is God's order: Thou shalt not kill. I beg you. I implore you. In the name of God, I command you. Stop the killing." The next week, while leading a Mass, Romero was shot dead.

American travelers mix it up with locals as the streets are filled to remember Romero.

The symbolic resurrection of Romero in his people is depicted in colorful murals showing the people of El Salvador rising like tall stocks of corn with big smiles and bullet wounds in their hands. In Latin America, crosses are decorated with peasants and symbols of their lives—healthy stocks of corn. While this is a land of martyrs, it's also a fertile land of resurrection.

During the repression of the 1970s and 1980s, many nuns and religious laywomen were murdered along with Romero. Their spirit, like Romero's, clearly lives on in the feisty women of the church so outspoken in El Salvador today.

Nuns we met had a passionate message and lots of quotable quotes: "Excluding and dehumanizing the poor is a kind of terrorism. Latin America has one of the biggest gaps between the rich and poor. As the gap grows, it's a kind of war. Hunger is violence. There can be no peace when there is still hunger. The push of globalization here has taught us that as humanity learns to worship the god of productivity, a

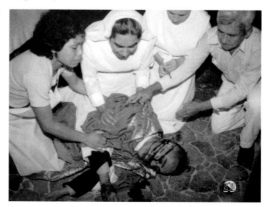

Archbishop Oscar Romero of El Salvador said, "If I am killed, I will be resurrected in my community." Today, he lives in his people, depicted here symbolically wearing his bullet holes.

civilization of hopelessness is being created. Suffering and sadness are not synonymous. Salvadorans laugh as hard as they cry. They love to say, 'If God wills, tomorrow will be better.' Here in El Salvador we believe that, on the day you meet your maker, you will be met by an angel to wipe away your tears. Woe to you who arrive with dry eyes."

Priests and nuns are routinely excommunicated in Central America for their political activism. While technically booted from their Church, they continue their work without missing a beat, believing, as one priest told me, "Part of our vow of obedience to the Church is disobedience to the Church."

Oscar Romero is not yet a saint. While the Vatican sends mixed signals, the local Catholic hierarchy is gradually trying to sanitize his image to be less offensive to the rich. But priests, nuns, and people throughout Central America are not waiting. For them, Oscar Romero is already "San Romero."

The University of Central America: Hotbed of Liberation Theology

We toured the University of Central America (UCA). While it felt like a humble college somewhere in Southern California, this place is a cultural and intellectual powerhouse in Central America. It was founded by San

Salvador's rich to give their children a safe and conservative environment for a higher education. It's run by Jesuits with the mission of giving students skills to make the world a better place.

Father Sobrino, who is on the faculty, told us the Jesuits' mission today: to create liberation architects, liberation mathematicians, and liberation teachers. UCA gets no money from the government and is no longer supported by the local elites. It relies on international aid. Because of their liberal teaching spirit, the Christmas packages from the wealthy to the professors stopped coming long ago...and the campus has been bombed 25 times.

Along with Sobrino, the school's six leading Jesuit professors were the intellectual leaders of Liberation Theology in the 1980s. That's why they

were considered leaders of the revolution. And that's why, in 1989, they were murdered. (Only Sobrino, who happened to be out of the country, survived.) We walked to a memorial garden where they were killed and heard the story.

Early one morning, the Jesuits were taken from their humble quarters and dragged into the garden. One by one they were shot in the brains with exploding bullets because they were the "brains of the people's movement." Before the government death squad left, they took time to shoot a bullet through the heart of a photo of Romero hanging on the wall...still trying to kill him nine years after his death.

Roses grow in a garden marking the place the six Jesuits were killed. The tomb of the six reads: "What it means to be a Jesuit in our time: to commit yourself to take risks in the crucial struggle of our age—the struggle for faith and the struggle for justice which that same faith demands. We will not work for the promotion of justice without paying a price."

Reading about events in faraway lands in the newspaper, you learn what happened. Then you can flip to the sports pages or comics. But hearing the story of an event from people who lived through it, you *feel* what happened. Right there behind the bedrooms of those professors, the smell of the flowers, the hard labor of the man bent over in the garden, the quiet focus of students whose parents lost a revolution, the knowledge that my country provided those exploding bullets...all combined to make this experience both vivid and enduring.

Lie Flat and Strum Your Guitar

Gathering at a hotel on the last night of our educational tour of El Salvador, we enjoyed a trio of guitarists. They were "100 percent popular" (the safe term used for anything perfectly in tune with the peoples' struggle). Enjoying their performance, I thought of the guerillas who once lay flat on the floors of their shacks under flying bullets. Strumming guitars quietly on their bellies, they sang forbidden songs. Music is the horse that carries the message of poems—weapons of a people's irrepressible spirit.

Listening to their music—love songs to their country—I stared at the musicians and considered the ongoing struggle. While troubadours sing of Christ's "preferential option for the poor," the forces of globalization relentlessly restructure Salvadoran society with a preferential option for the wealthy. Watching those slender Latino fingers crawl between the frets like guerillas quietly loping through the jungle, I thought of the courageous advocates of the people throughout the developing world, not running from the forces of globalization but engaging them.

They sang, "Our way of life is being erased...no more *huevos picados*, we now have omelets...no more *colones*, we now have dollars." They wondered musically, "How can a combo meal at a fast-food chain cost $8, while $20 gathered at church feeds 200 hungry mouths? Why did God put me here?"

Behind me sat Fernando Cardenal, white and grandfatherly in his well-worn blue jeans. As the minister of education of Nicaragua's revolutionary Sandinista government back in the 1980s, he fought the US and lost. Today his country—the revolution purged from its economy—is even poorer than El Salvador. But his bright eyes nodded to the beat and message of this new generation's musical call to action.

Wrapping up my El Salvador visit with this inspirational concert, I considered how the superstars of nonviolence (Gandhi, Martin Luther King Jr.,

John Lennon, Oscar Romero) all seem to get shot. Are the pacifists losers? As a competitive person, I don't like this idea. My 1988 visit to Central America was filled with hope. I came again after the defeat of people's movements in both El Salvador and Nicaragua in 1991. The tide had turned, and I wondered how the spirit of the people's movements—so exuberant just three years before—would fare after the American-funded victories in their domestic struggles. Then, in 2005, after 14 years of globalization, it was clear—there was only one game in town. Sure, Romero lives…and Jesus lives. And half the world is trying to live, too…on that two bucks a day. As a Christian, I like to see religion function as a liberator rather than an opiate. Perhaps that's why I am so enamored with Liberation Theology in Central America, and why travel here impacts my worldview so powerfully.

Refocusing on the troubadours, I heard them sing, "It's not easy to see God in the child who cleans the windshields at a San Salvador intersection… but we must."

Chapter 5
Denmark: Highly Taxed and Highly Content

Traveling through Denmark, I enjoy a constant barrage of experiences that give me food for political thought. This most highly taxed corner of Europe likes its system. An exceptionally affluent society, it chooses to sip rather than to gulp. It's a traditionally blonde corner of Europe that struggles with immigration issues. And Copenhagen's famous hippie commune, now nearly 40 years old, is standing strong against a rising tide of free market trends.

There's plenty in Denmark that Americans who travel as students of the world can ponder in order to spice up their take on well-worn social and economic issues back home. This chapter delves into a few of the joys and challenges of Danish life. It also serves as a practical example of how one European country embraces that continent's more socialistic system and faces the immigration challenges that I discussed in Chapter 3. This snapshot of Danish life is a reminder that you can glean powerful lessons even when you travel to more comfortable countries that don't seem so different from back home.

Everything's So...Danish

Wherever you travel, you encounter societies that are driven by a desire for their people to live well. Denmark seems particularly adept at this feat. In survey after survey, when asked whether they're content with their lives, the Danes are routinely found to be among the happiest people on earth. With each visit to Denmark, it's become my mission to figure out: What makes those Danes so darned happy?

Expensive, highly taxed, and highly efficient Denmark confuses me. The affluence of Denmark's Scandinavian cousin in Norway can be explained by their North Sea oil bonanza. But the Danes' leading natural resources are wind power, pigs, and pickled herring. Considering the very high cost of living here, the Danish lifestyle seems richer than their modest after-tax incomes would suggest. In fact, the Danes live extremely well. Traveling through what seems to be a fantasy land, you keep wondering, "How do they do it?"

First off, there's the obvious: Denmark is, simply, pleasant. I'm impressed by how serene things are, even in the bustling capital of Copenhagen. Their new subway is silent, automated, on the honor system (with random ticket checks rather than turnstiles), and trains go literally every two minutes. The streets are so quiet (thanks to downtown pedestrian-only zones) that I don't yell to my friends from a distance…I walk over to speak to them in a soft "indoors voice." On my last visit, I saw an angry young man at the Copenhagen train station barking into his mobile phone—and it occurred to me that in a week in the country, that was the only shouting I'd heard.

When you get beyond Copenhagen and travel into the Danish countryside, you find yourself saying "cute" a lot. Thatched-roof farms dot a green

landscape of rolling hills and fields. Sailboats bob in tiny harbors. Parents push kids in prams along pedestrian-only streets. Copper spires create fairy-tale skylines. The place feels like a pitch 'n putt course sparsely inhabited by blonde Vulcans. Travelers here find the human scale and orderliness of Danish society itself the focus of their sightseeing. Everything is just so…Danish.

The local Disneyland—Legoland—is a wildly popular place featuring 58 million Lego bricks built into famous landmarks from around the world. (They claim that if you lined them all up, they'd stretch from here to Italy.) The place is crawling with adorable little ice-cream-licking, blonde children. Although stoked with piles of sugar, the scene is strikingly mellow. Kids hold their mothers' hands while learning about the Lego buildings and smile contentedly as they circle around on the carousel.

Riding Danish trains is also thought-provoking. Wandering into a nearly empty, sleek train car, I noticed that each seat was marked *Kan reserveres.* I figured that meant "not reserved," and sat down. Then I was bumped by a friendly Dane with a reservation. He said, "The sign means the seat 'could be' reserved...we don't promise too much." Noticing several young men with shaved heads and the finest headphones listening to iPods as they made clockwork connections on their commute to work, I thought that Denmark seemed so minimalistic and efficient...and so well-ordered.

On another train ride, I was filming a segment for a public television show. I'd look into the camera and say, "A fun part of exploring Denmark is enjoying the efficiency of the great train system." As usual, I needed about six or eight "takes" to get it right. My Danish friend was chuckling the whole time. He finally explained that our train was running eight minutes late, and each time I said my line, all the Danes on the train around me would mutter, "No, no, no." Clearly, it's all relative. While only two trains a day serve my town back home, these trains go six times an hour. And while many Danes go through life without ever getting around to buying a car, they still grouse about things like public transit. My friend said, "We Danes are spoiled. We love to complain."

Danish "Social-ism" and the Free Rider Problem

Of course, there's much more to Danish contentedness than being quaint and orderly. It's all built upon a firm cultural foundation. Danish society seems to be a finely tuned social internal-combustion engine in a glass box: highly taxed, highly connected, and highly regulated, with all the gears properly engaged. Their system is a hybrid that, it seems, has evolved as far as socialism can go without violating the necessary fundamentals of capitalism and democracy. It's socialistic...but, with its unique emphasis on society, it's also social-istic.

What happens when a tune-up is needed? My Danish friends tell me they rely on their government. Rather than doing what's best for corporations, the Danish government clearly looks out for the people's interests. The Danes say, "If our government lets us down, we let ourselves down."

This strong social ethic permeates the whole of Danish society. A traveler can find it in its raw and indigenous form in the rural corners and small towns—places where anyone is allowed to pick berries and nuts, but "no more than would fit in your hat."

On a recent visit to a Danish small town, I saw this social ethic in the way a local friend of mine reacted to a controversy. The biggest hotel in his town started renting bikes to compete with Mrs. Hansen's bike rental shop. My friend was disappointed in the hotel manager, saying, "They don't need to do that—bike rental has been Mrs. Hansen's livelihood since she was a little girl." Of course, there's no law forbidding it. And with our American business ethic, we'd just say that competition is good. But in Denmark, to look out for Mrs. Hansen's little bike rental business was a matter of neighborly decency.

Other countries have struggled to become more social-istic...and failed. So how do the Danes pull it off? I think their success relates to their accep-

Immigrants: Treasure Your Heritage...and Melt

I've painted a rosy picture of Denmark. But the country is not without its challenges. One key issue facing Denmark, along with the rest of Europe and the US, is immigration.

These days, incentives for immigrants to blend quickly are not as strong as when my grandparents sailed to America from Norway. Thanks to modern telecommunications advances, communities of foreigners can settle in more comfortable places while remaining in close contact with friends and family back home. Like the Algerian family I mentioned in Chapter 3 (who've been in the Netherlands for three generations, speak barely a word of Dutch, and are still enthusiastically Algerian), these people have no interest in assimilating. Consequently, rather than "melting pots," wealthy countries such as Denmark are becoming cafeteria plates with dividers keeping ethnic groups separate.

Immigration can be a major wedge issue—especially in formerly homogenous nations. Only 40 years ago, there were virtually no foreigners in Denmark. As in many European countries, part of the population, especially older and more insular Danes, fears immigrants and gravitates to right-wing, racist parties. Meanwhile, progressive Danes—who celebrate a multicultural future—wonder why their wealthy nation of high-tech, multilingual globalists is still struggling to get along with their relatively small community of Muslim immigrants. While some Danes view their growing Muslim minority as a problem, others are willing to see a more colorful society as an opportunity.

At Copenhagen's City Museum, I met a Pakistani Dane who worked there as a guide. He spoke Danish like a local and talked earnestly about the

tance of their social contract. Any society needs to subscribe to a social contract—basically, what you agree to give up in order to live together peacefully. Densely populated Europe generally embraces Rousseau's social contract: In order to get along well, everyone will contribute a little more than their share and give up a little more than their share. Then, together, we'll all be fine.

The Danes—who take this mindset to the extreme—are particularly conscientious about not exploiting loopholes. They are keenly aware of the so-called "free rider problem": If you knew you could get away with it, would you do something to get more than your fair share? The Danes recognize that if everyone did this, their system would collapse. Therefore, they don't. It seems to me that the Danes make choices considering what would happen to their society (not just to themselves) if *everyone* cheated on this, sued someone for that, freeloaded here, or ignored that rule there.

A Muslim Dane catches the changing of her country's guard.

exhibit, as if his own ancestors pioneered the city. Thinking of assimilation, I got emotional. Surprised at being choked up, I was struck by the beauty of a Pakistani Dane as opposed to a Pakistani living in Denmark.

Am I wrong to wish that a Muslim living in Denmark would become a Dane? Am I wrong to wish the US would speak only English, rather than Norwegian or Spanish as well? Am I wrong to lament districts of London that have a disdain for all things British? Immigrants energize a land—but they do it best (as is the story of the US) when their vision is a healthy melting pot. Melt, immigrants...treasure your heritage while embracing your adopted homelands. But it's more than just an "immigrant issue." Europeans (like Americans) fearful of encroachment, change, and differing hues of skin need to show tolerance, outreach, and understanding. From what I've seen, with these attitudes, it works better for all involved.

In contrast, the United States subscribes to John Locke's version of the social contract: a "don't fence me in" ideal of rugged individualism, where you can do anything you like as long as you don't hurt your neighbor. Just keep the government off our backs. In some ways, this suits us: As we have always had more elbow room, we can get away with our independent spirit. Thanks to our wide-open spaces, determination to be self-sufficient, and relative population sparsity, it's easier—and arguably less disruptive—for us to ignore the free rider problem.

If I had to identify one major character flaw of Americans, it might be our inability to appreciate the free rider problem. Many Americans practically consider it their birthright to make money they didn't really earn, enjoy the fruits of our society while cheating on their taxes, drive a gas-guzzler just because they can afford it, take up two parking spots so no one will bump their precious car, and generally jigger the system if they can get away with it. We often seem to consider actions like these acceptable...without considering the fact that if everyone did it, our society as a whole would suffer.

The consequences of ignoring this reality were thrown into sharp relief with the crippling financial crisis that began in 2008. In the lead-up to the crisis, smart people knew deep down that existing policies would not be sustainable if everyone jumped in, trying to make money from speculation rather than substance. They gambled that they could pull it off, and the free rider problem wouldn't kick it. But then it did. As Europe, too, got caught up in this "casino capitalism," we saw how interconnected our world has become, and how—with the globalization of our economies—there's now only one game in town.

A good example of how the Danish social ethic differs from others is a simple one: Danes are famous for not jaywalking. Even if the roads are empty at 3 a.m., pedestrians still stop and wait at a red light. If there's no traffic in sight, my American individualism whispers, "Why obey a silly rule?" And so I jaywalk, boldly, assuming that my fellow pedestrians will appreciate my lead and follow me. In most countries, they do. But when I jaywalk in Denmark, the locals frown at me like I'm a bad influence on the children present. That social pressure impacts even a hurried, jaywalking tourist. So, rather than feel like an evil person, I wait for the light.

I don't know how well I'd fit in if I lived in Denmark. But their personal and societal formula intrigues me. On my last visit, I asked Danish people I met about their society—and why they're so happy. Here's a sampling of what they told me:

"Yes, we are the most contented people. Regular workers pay on average 50 percent taxes—big shots pay up to 70 percent. Of course, we expect and we get a good value for our taxes. We've had national healthcare since the 1930s. We know nothing else. If I don't like the shape of my nose, I pay to fix that. But all my basic health needs are taken care of. Here in Denmark, all education is free. And our taxes even provide university students with $800 a month for living expenses for up to six years. We Danes believe a family's economic status should have nothing to do with two fundamental rights: the quality of their healthcare or the quality of the education their children receive. I believe you in America pay triple per person what we pay as a society for healthcare. Your system may be better for business…but ours is better for people. Perhaps a major negative consequence of our socialism is that since Danes are so accustomed to everything being taken care of by the government, we may not be very helpful or considerate towards each other when in need."

When I saw a tombstone store with *Tak for Alt* ("Thanks for Everything") pre-carved into each headstone, I figured it was a message from the dearly departed after enjoying a very blessed life in Denmark. But I asked a Dane, and learned that it's a message from the living bidding their loved one farewell (similar to our "Rest in Peace"). Still, I think when a Dane dies, it's a good message from both sides: *Tak for Alt.*

Living Large While Living Small

An interesting side effect of the Danish system is that sky-high taxes make things so costly that people consume more sparingly. The society seems designed in a way that encourages people to use less, waste less, chew slower, appreciate more, and just sip things. A glass of beer can cost $10. A cup of coffee can run $7—and refills are unheard of. A big box economy à la Wal-Mart is just not very Danish. I think Danes know they could make more money if they embraced the "Big Gulp" track and started super-sizing things. But the collective decision is based on what's good for the fabric of their society rather than what's good for the economy.

One example that's obvious to any visitor is cars…or the lack thereof. Figuring in registration fees and sales tax, Denmark levies a nearly 200 percent tax on new automobiles. So to buy one car, you have to pay for three cars. As a result, throughout Denmark, a third dimension zips along silently between pedestrians and drivers: Danish bikers. With so many bikes, traffic congestion and pollution are reduced, parked cars don't clog the streets, and people are in shape. (What's safe for the environment can be dangerous for absentminded pedestrians. On my last visit to Copenhagen, on two occasions I was nearly flattened as I stepped from a taxi into the bike lane.)

London and Paris have taken lanes away from drivers to create bike lanes, but so far the lanes are underused and the entire effort just seems to make things worse. Somehow, Copenhagen has it figured out. During Copenhagen's rush hour, there are more bikes on their roads than cars, and everything moves smoothly.

While walking through one of Copenhagen's main squares, I noticed it was dominated by people, cobbles, and buildings. It felt calm, spacious, and inviting. I looked again and saw that there were also about fifty bikes—blending into the scene almost unnoticed—and absolutely no cars. If instead of bikes, those were parked cars, the charm would be gone.

Hotels have even started providing visiting guests with loaner or rental bikes. I find having a bike parked in my hotel's bike rack is a great way to fit in and literally "go local." Copenhagen has as many bike lanes as car lanes, and I can get anywhere in the town center as fast on my two wheels as by taxi. When you get out of the city to explore the Danish countryside, you'll see that newly paved roads are lined by perfectly smooth bike lanes—one for each direction. Even out in the country, it seems that bikes outnumber cars.

You'll see more bikes than cars on Copenhagen's squares.

Christiania: Copenhagen's Embattled Commune

I was strolling through the commotion of downtown Copenhagen, past chain restaurants dressed up to look old and under towering hotels that seem to sport the name of a different international chain each year. Then, as if from another age, a man pedaled by me with his wife sitting in the utilitarian bucket-like wagon of his three-wheeled "Christiania Bike." You'd call the couple "granola" in the US.

Looking as out of place here in Copenhagen as an Amish couple wandering the canyons of Manhattan, they were residents of Christiania.

The Denmark I've described seems to be a model of conformity, where everyone obeys the laws so that all can be safe, affluent, and comfortable. And yet, Denmark also hosts Europe's most inspirational and thriving nonconformist hippie commune. Perhaps being content and conformist is easier for a society when its nonconformist segment, rebelling against all that buttoned-down conformity, has a refuge.

In 1971, the original 700 Christianians established squatters' rights in an abandoned military barracks just

Copenhagen's Christiania—a squatters' commune since 1971.

a 10-minute walk from the Danish parliament building. A generation later, this "free city" still stands—an ultra-human communal mishmash of idealists, hippies, potheads, non-materialists, and happy children (600 adults, 200 kids, 200 cats, 200 dogs, 17 horses, and a couple of parrots). Seeing seniors with gray ponytails woodworking, tending their gardens, and serving as guardians of the community's ideals, I'm reminded that 180 of the original gang that took over the barracks four decades ago still call Christiania home. The Christianians are fighting a rising tide of materialism and conformity. They want to raise their children to be not cogs, but free spirits.

Everyone knows utopias are utopian—they can't work. But Christiania, which has evolved with the challenges of making a utopia a viable reality, acts like it didn't get the message. It's broken into 14 administrative neighborhoods on land still owned by Denmark's Ministry of Defense. Locals build their homes but don't own the land; there's no buying or selling of property. When someone moves out, the community decides who will be invited in to replace that person. A third of the adult population works on the outside, a third works on the inside, and a third doesn't work much at all.

For the first few years, hard drugs and junkies were tolerated. But that led to violence and polluted the mellow ambience residents envisioned. In 1979, the junkies were expelled—an epic confrontation now embedded in the community's folk history. Since then, the symbol of a fist breaking a syringe is as prevalent as the leafy marijuana icon. Hard drugs are emphatically forbidden in Christiania.

Christiania says yes to marijuana and no to hard drugs.

Marijuana has always been the national plant of the free city. "Pusher Street" (named for the former sale of soft drugs here) is Christiania's main drag. In recent years, to pre-empt city forces shutting down the entire community for its open sale of pot, residents bulldozed the marijuana stalls lining Pusher Street. (In spite of regular police raids, marijuana remains prevalent. But the retailing, while still fragrant, is no longer flagrant.)

Because of its current crackdown, Copenhagen is experiencing firsthand a classic case study in the regrettable consequences of a war on marijuana. For the first time in years, the Copenhagen street price for pot is up, gangs are moving into the marijuana business, and crime is associated with pot.

There was actually a murder in 2005, as pushers fought to establish their turf—almost unthinkable in Copenhagen before the stalls along Pusher Street were bulldozed. (For more on marijuana, see Chapter 7.)

Get beyond the touristy main drag of Christiania, and you'll find a fascinating, ramshackle world of peaceniks shuffled with some irony among the moats, earthen ramparts, and barracks of the former military base. Alternative housing, carpenter shops, hippie villas, cozy tea houses, children's playgrounds, peaceful lanes, and interfaith stupa-like temples serve people who believe that "to be normal is to be in a straightjacket."

There are a handful of basic rules: no cars, no hard drugs, no guns, no explosives, and so on. A few "luxury hippies" have oil heat, but most use wood or gas. The community has one mailing address. A phone chain provides a system of communal security because, as people there report, they've had bad experiences calling the police. As a reminder of the constant police presence lately, my favorite Christiania café, Månefiskeren ("Moon Fisher"), has a sign outside saying: "The world's safest café—police raids nearly every day."

And an amazing thing has happened: Christiania—famous for its counterculture scene, geodesic domes on its back streets, and vegetarian cafés—has become the third-most-visited sight among tourists in Copenhagen. Move over, *Little Mermaid.*

I recently got an email from some traveling readers. They said, "We're not prudes, but Christiania was creepy. Don't take kids here or go after dark."

I agree. The free city is not pretty. But hanging out with parents raising their children with Christiania values, and sharing a meal featuring homegrown vegetables with a couple born and raised in this community, I found a distinct human beauty in the place. And I came to believe more strongly than ever that it's important to allow this social experiment and give alternative-type people a place to live out their values.

As I biked through Christiania, it also occurred to me that, except for the bottled beer being sold, there was not a hint of any corporate entity in the entire "free city." There was no advertising and no big business. Everything was handmade. Nothing was packaged. People consumed as if how they spent their money shaped the environment in which they lived and raised their families. It's not such a far cry from their fellow Danes, who also see themselves as conscientious participants in society.

But ever since its inception, Christiania has been a political hot potato. No one in the Danish establishment wanted it. And no one has had the nerve to mash it. While once very popular with the general Copenhagen community, Christianians have lost some goodwill recently as they are seen more as a clique, no longer accepting others to join and looking out only for themselves. Mindful of their need for popular support from their Copenhagen neighbors, Christianians are working to connect better with the rest of society. Its residents now pool their money, creating a fund to pay for utilities and city taxes (about $1 million a year) and an annual budget of about $1 million to run their local affairs.

But Denmark's relatively conservative government is trying to "normalize" Christiania, pressured by developers salivating at the potential profits of developing this once nearly worthless land, and by the US because of the residents' celebrated open use of marijuana. Increasingly, this community of peaceniks is in danger of being evicted.

By way of compromise, there's talk about opening Christiania to 1,600 residents who aren't part of the commune and developing posh apartments to replace existing residences. Injecting outsiders and market forces into the last attempt at a socialist utopia surviving in Europe from its flower-power days is designed to (and likely will) bring great change.

As I left Christiania and headed back into clean, orderly, and con-

With little money, advertising, or styles to keep up with, Christianians do a lot of swapping.

formist Denmark, I looked up at the back side of the "Welcome to Christiania" sign. It read, "You are entering the EU."

Later that day on the bustling streets of downtown Copenhagen, I paused to watch a parade of ragtag soldiers-against-conformity dressed in black and waving "Save Christiania" banners. They walked sadly behind a WWII-vintage truck blasting Pink Floyd's "Another Brick in the Wall." (I had never really listened to the words before. But the anthem of self-imposed isolation and revolt against conformity seemed to perfectly fit the determination of the Christianians to stand up against thought control and stifled individuality.) On their banner, a slogan—painted onto an old bedsheet—read: *Lev livet kunstnerisk! Kun døde fisk flyder med strømmen* ("Live life artistically! Only dead fish follow the current"). Those marching flew the Christiania flag—three yellow dots on an orange background. They say the dots are from the o's in "Love Love Love."

While I wouldn't choose to live in Christiania, I would feel a loss if it were shut down. There's something unfortunately brutal about a world that makes the little Christianias—independent bookstores, family farms, nomadic communities, and so on—fight giants (such as developers, big chains, agribusiness, and centralized governments) to the death. Those economic and governmental behemoths always seem to win. And when they do, we may become safer and wealthier and even more comfortable...but it all comes at a cost.

The need for a Christiania is not limited to the Danes. After that trip, from the comfort of my suburban Seattle living room, I stumbled upon live TV coverage of the finale of the Burning Man Festival (the annual massing of America's artistic free spirits each Labor Day in the Nevada desert). Watching it, I heard the cry of an American fringe community that—much like the tribe at Christiania—wants to be free in an increasingly interconnected world that demands conformity.

Traveling in Denmark, considering well-ordered Danish social-ism and reflecting on the free-spirited ideals and struggles of Christiania, gives me insight into parts of my own society that refuse to be just another brick in the wall. Hopefully when the pressures of conformity require selling a bit of our soul, travel experiences like these help us understand the potential loss before it's regrettably gone.

Denmark is a riddle that I love puzzling over. On the one hand, their dedication to their social contract is the bedrock of their insistent happiness. On the other, in their longstanding acceptance of Christiania, the Danes seem to be unusually tolerant of free spirits. I imagine that the dramatic tension between these extremes is part of what keeps Danish life interesting... both for the Danes and for us visitors. As all societies vie to win the "most contented" surveys, traveling reminds us that contentment is based not on surrendering to conformity, but in finding that balance between working well together and letting creative spirits run free.

Chapter 6
Turkey and Morocco: Sampling Secular Islam

M y Dad used to be absolutely distraught by the notion that God and Allah could be the same. I couldn't resist teaching our son, Andy (when he was about three years old), to hold out his arms, bob them up and down, and say, "Allah, Allah, Allah" after table grace just to freak out his Grandpa. Later, rather than just torture my Dad, I took a more loving (and certainly more effective) approach to opening him up to the Muslim world: I took him to Turkey. Now—while he's still afraid of Osama's gang—my Dad is no longer afraid of Islam.

While violent Islamic fundamentalists represent a tiny fraction of all Muslims, the threats they pose are real. And they get plenty of media coverage. To help balance my understanding of Islam, I make a point to travel to and learn about its reasonable, mainstream side. I spend time in Turkey, a Western-facing Islamic nation with a determination to stay secular and a desire to engage the US and Europe as friends without giving up its culture. Morocco is another good classroom for gaining a balanced take on Islam. Visiting moderate developing nations like these, which happen to be primarily Muslim, gives us an accessible look at a fast-growing religion of 1.3 billion people worldwide. We can observe Islamic societies struggling (like our own society) with how to deal with a rough-and-tumble globalized world. In doing so, we gain empathy.

Turkey is also a good classroom in which to better understand our world because it gives us a peek at an emerging economy. With the frailties of the US economy and the G-8 stretching to G-20, it's smart to pay attention to the globe's new economic realities. Turkey—with its torrid modernization, its drift to the political right, and the rise of Islamic fundamentalism—is a study in the cultural schizophrenia that modern change can cause, from Mumbai to Memphis.

The predictable question travelers get from loved ones is, "Why are you going to Turkey?" With each visit to Istanbul, one of my favorite cities in the world, my response is: Why would anyone not travel here?

Istanbul Déjà Vu

When I was in my twenties, I finished eight European trips in a row in Turkey. I didn't plan it that way—it was the natural finale, the subconscious cherry on top of every year's travel adventures. While my passion for Turkey hasn't faded, my ability to spend time there has been a casualty of my busy schedule researching guidebooks and producing public television shows. But recently, realizing I hadn't set foot in Istanbul for nearly a decade, I made a point to return to the city where East meets West. The comforting similarities and jarring differences between today's Istanbul and the Istanbul I remember filled the trip both with nostalgia and with vivid examples of how change is sweeping the planet.

The moment I stepped off my plane, I remembered how much I enjoy this country. Marveling at the efficiency of Istanbul's Atatürk Airport, I popped onto the street and into a yellow *taksi*. Seeing the welcoming grin of the unshaven driver who greeted me with a "*Merhaba*," I just blurted out, "*Çok güzel.*" I forgot I remembered the phrase. It just came to me—like a baby shouts for joy. I was back in Turkey, and it was "very beautiful" indeed. My first hours in Turkey were filled with similar déjà vu moments like no travel homecoming I could remember.

As the *taksi* turned off the highway and into the tangled lanes of the tourist zone—just below the Blue Mosque—all the tourist-friendly businesses were still lined up, providing a backdrop for their chorus line of barkers shouting, "Yes, Mister!"

I looked at the dirty kids in the streets and remembered a rougher time, when kids like these would earn small change by hanging out the passenger door of ramshackle vans. They'd yell "Topkapı, Topkapı, Topkapı" (or whichever neighborhood was the destination) in a scramble to pick up passengers in the shared minibuses called *dolmuş*. (The *dolmuş*—a wild cross between a taxi, a bus, and a kidnapping vehicle—is literally and so appropriately called "stuffed").

While Turkey's new affluence has nearly killed the *dolmuş*, the echoes of the boys hollering from the vans bounced happily in my memory: "Aksaray, Aksaray, Aksaray...Sultanahmet, Sultanahmet, Sultanahmet." I remembered my favorite call was for the train station's neighborhood: "Sirkeci, Sirkeci, Sirkeci."

Istanbul, a city of over 10 million, is thriving. The city is poignantly littered both with remnants of grand (if eventually corrupt) empires and with living, breathing reminders of the harsh reality of life in the developing world. Sipping my tea, I watched old men shuffle by, hunched over as if still

Like great cities in emerging economies around the world, Istanbul bustles with hope for a bright future.

bent under the towering loads they had carried all of their human-beast-of-burden lives.

And yet, this ancient city is striding into the future. During my visit, everyone was buzzing about the upcoming completion of the new tunnel under the Bosphorus, which would give a million commuters in the Asian suburbs of Istanbul an easy train link to their places of work in Europe. This tunnel is emblematic of modern Turkey's commitment to connecting East and West, just as Istanbul bridges Asia and Europe. I also see it as a concrete example of how parts of the developing world are emerging as economic dynamos.

Stepping out of my shoes, I entered the vast and turquoise (and therefore not-quite-rightly-named) Blue Mosque. Hoping for another déjà vu, I didn't get it. Something was missing. Yes…gone was the smell of countless sweaty socks, knees, palms, and foreheads soaked into the ancient carpet upon which worshippers did their quite physical prayer work-outs. Sure enough, the Blue Mosque had a fresh new carpet—with a subtle design that keeps worshippers organized the same way that lined paper tames printed letters.

The prayer service let out, and a sea of Turks surged for the door. Being caught up in a crush of locals—where the only way to get any personal space is to look up—is a connecting-with-humanity ritual for me. I seek out these opportunities. It's the closest I'll ever come to experiencing the exhilaration of body-surfing above a mosh pit. Going outside with the worshipping flow, I scanned the dark sky. That scene—one I had forgotten was so breathtaking—played for me again: hard-pumping seagulls powering through the humid air in a black sky, surging into the light as they crossed in front of floodlit minarets.

Walking down to the Golden Horn inlet and Istanbul's churning waterfront, I crossed the new Galata Bridge, which made me miss the dismantled and shipped-out old Galata Bridge—so crusty with life's struggles. Feeling a wistful nostalgia, I thought of how all societies morph with the push and pull of the times.

But then I realized that, while the old bridge is gone, the new one has been engulfed with the same vibrant street life—boys casting their lines, old men sucking on water pipes, and sesame-seed bread rings filling cloudy glass-windowed carts.

Strolling the new Galata Bridge and still finding old scenes reminded me how stubborn cultural inertia can be. If you give a camel-riding Bedouin a new Mercedes, he still decorates it like a camel. I remember looking at tribal leaders in Afghanistan—shaved, cleaned up, and given a bureaucrat's uniform. But looking more closely, I could see the bushy-gray-bearded men in dusty old robes still living behind those modern uniforms. On a trip to Kathmandu, I recall seeing a Californian who had dropped out of the "modern rat race"—calloused almost-animal feet, matted dreadlocks, draped in sackcloth as he stood, cane in hand, before the living virgin goddess. Somehow I could still see Los Angeles in his eyes. The resilience of a culture can't be overcome with a haircut and a shave—or lack of one—or a new bridge.

On the sloppy adjacent harborfront, the venerable "fish and bread boats" were still rocking in the constant chop of the busy harbor. In a humbler day, they were 20-foot-long open dinghies—rough boats with battered car tires for fenders—with open fires for grilling fish literally fresh off the boat. For a few coins, the fishermen would bury a big white fillet in a hunk of fluffy white bread, wrap it in newsprint, and I was on my way…dining out on fish.

In recent years, the fish and bread boats had been shut down—they had no license. After a popular uproar, they came back. They're a bit more hygienic, no longer using newspaper for wrapping, but still rocking in the waves and slamming out fresh fish.

In Turkey, I have more personal rituals than in other countries. I cap my days with a bowl of *sütlaç*. That's rice pudding with a sprinkle of cinnamon—

still served in a square and shiny stainless-steel bowl with a matching spoon, not much bigger than a gelato sampler.

And I don't let a day go by in Turkey without enjoying a teahouse game of backgammon with a stranger. Boards have become less characteristic; they're now cheap and mass-produced, almost disposable. Today's dice—plastic and perfect—make me miss the tiny handmade "bones" of the 20th century, with their disobedient dots. But some things never change. To test a fun cultural quirk, I tossed my dice and paused. As I remembered, a bystander moved for me. When it comes to backgammon, there's one right way…and everybody knows it. And in Turkey, as if a result of its ruthless history, when starting a new game, the winner goes first.

With each backgammon game, I think of one of my most precious possessions back home: an old-time, hand-hewn, inlaid backgammon board, with rusty little hinges held in place by hasty tacks, and soft, white wood worn deeper than the harder, dark wood. Twenty years after taking that backgammon board home, I open it and still smell the tobacco, tea, and soul of a traditional Turkish community. There's almost nothing in my world that is worn or has been enjoyed long enough to absorb the smells of my life and community. It's a reminder to me of the cost of modernity. And when the feel and smell of my old backgammon board takes me back to Turkey, I'm reminded how, in the face of all that modernity, the resilient charm of traditional cultures is endangered and worth preserving.

Today in Turkey, the people—like those dots on the modern dice—line up better. The weave of a mosque carpet provides direction. There's a seat for everyone, as the *dolmus* are no longer so stuffed. Fez sales to tourists are way down, but scarf wear by local women (a symbol of traditional Muslim identity) is way up. Each of my déjà vu moments shows a society confronting powerful forces of change while also wanting to stay the same.

My hotel's inviting terrace was open at night, ideal for gazing past floodlit husks of forts and walls, out at the sleepy Bosphorus, with Asia lurking just across the inky straits. The strategic waterway was speckled with the lights of freighters at anchor stretching far into the distance.

Noticing the power of the moonlight shimmering on the water, I recalled the legend of the Turkish flag—a white star and crescent moon reflected in a pool of bright-red blood after a great and victorious battle. From my perch, it seemed that now the crescent moon shone over not blood, but money: trade and shipping…modern-day battles in the arena of capitalism.

At breakfast, the same view was lively, and already bright enough to make me wish I had sunglasses. An empty oil tanker heading for a Romanian fill-up was light and riding high. Its exposed tank made its prow cut through the water like a plow—a reminder of how, today, trade is sustenance and oil is a treasured crop. As I scanned the city, it occurred to me that Istanbul is

physically not that different from my home city. I could replace the skyline of domed mosques and minarets with churches and spires, and it could be the rough end of Any Port City, USA.

Rather than my standard bowl of cereal, for my Turkish breakfasts I go local—olives, goat cheese, cucumbers, tomatoes, bread, and a horrible instant orange drink masquerading as juice. Gazing at my plate, I studied the olive oil. Ignoring the three olive pits, I saw tiny, mysterious flakes of spices. They were doing a silent and slow-motion do-si-do to a distant rhythm with lyrics that told of arduous camel-caravan rides along the fabled Silk Road from China.

Later that day, I immersed myself in Turkey, collecting random memories. Wandering under stiletto minarets, I listened as a hardworking loudspeaker—lashed to the minaret as if a religious crow's nest—belted out a call to prayer. Noticing the twinkling lights strung up in honor of the holy month of Ramadan, I thought, "Charming—they've draped Christmas lights between the minarets." But a Turk might come to my house and say,

"Charming—he's draped Ramadan lights on his Christmas tree." I marveled at the multigenerational conviviality at the Hippodrome—that long, oblong plaza still shaped like the chariot racecourse it was 18 centuries ago. Precocious children high-fived me and tried out their only English phrase: "What is your name?" Just to enjoy their quizzical look, I'd say, "Seven o'clock." As I struggle to understand their society, I guess my mischievous streak wanted them to deal with a little confusion as well.

It's in this environment that, as a tour guide, I would introduce tour members (like my father) to Turkish culture and Islam. I recall well-educated professionals struggling to get things straight. People would quiz me: "So, where did they get the name Quran for their Bible? Could it be considered a Bible?" Turkish guides love to tell stories of tourists who ask, "So, was this church built before or after Christ?" But all guides repeat to themselves the first rule of guiding: "There are no stupid questions." After all, it's in environments like Istanbul—in countries all around the world—that thoughtful travelers get out of their comfort zones and enjoy the easy educational rewards that come with being steep on the learning curve.

Turkish Village Insights in Güzelyurt

Big cities can be relatively cosmopolitan and homogenized by modern affluence. But small towns, with their more change-averse residents, are cultural humidors—keeping fragile traditions moist and full of local flavor.

Güzelyurt, an obscure-to-the-world but proud-of-itself village in central Turkey, teaches me the richness and nobility of rustic village life in the developing world. Students of the world find that, in any country, remote towns and villages can be wonderful classrooms.

Güzelyurt was all decked out on my last visit. I happened to arrive on the day of everybody's favorite festival: a circumcision party. Turks call it "a wedding without the in-laws." The little boy, dressed like a prince, rode tall on his decorated donkey through a commotion of friends and relatives to the house where a doctor was sharpening his knife. Even with paper money pinned to his fancy outfit and loved ones chanting calming spiritual music, the boy looked frightened. But the ritual snipping went off without a glitch—and a good time was had at least by everyone else.

On a different trip, I learned that Turkish weddings—while not as much fun as circumcisions—are also quite a spectacle. I'll never forget being a special guest at a wedding in Güzelyurt. The entire community gathered.

Calling the party to order, the oldest couple looked happily at the young bride and groom and shared a local blessing: "May you grow old together on one pillow."

Whenever there's a family festival, village Turks turn on the music and dance. Everybody is swept onto their feet—including visiting tourists. It's easy: Just follow the locals as they hold out their arms, snap their fingers, and shake their shoulders. During one such Güzelyurt party, the man of the house came over to me—the foreigner—and wanted to impress me. Waving me to a quiet corner, he said, "Here on my wall, the most sacred place in my home, is my Quran bag, where I keep my Quran. And in my Quran bag I also keep a copy of the Bible and a copy of the Torah—because I believe that we Muslims, Christians, and Jews are all 'children of the Book'…children of the same good God."

Leaving the party, I walked down the street. The town seemed cluttered with ugly unfinished concrete buildings bristling with rusty reinforcement bars. While I love the Turks, I couldn't help but think, "Why can't these people get their act together and just finish these buildings?" That was before I learned that in Turkey, there's an ethic among parents—even poor ones—that you leave your children with a house. Historically Turks are reluctant to store money in the bank because it disappears through inflation. So instead, they invest bit by bit by constructing a building. Every time they get a hundred bucks together, they put it into that ever-growing house.

They leave the rebar exposed until they have another hundred bucks, so they make another wall, put on a window, frame in another door...and add more rebar. Now, when I look at that rusty rebar, I remember that Turks say, "Rebar holds the family together."...and it becomes much prettier.

At the edge of Güzelyurt, I came upon a little boy playing a flute. Just like in biblical times, it was carved out of an eagle bone. I listened. And I heard another eagle-bone flute, out of sight, coming from over the hill, where his dad was tending the sheep. As they have for centuries, the boy stays with the mom and plays the eagle-bone flute. The dad tends the flock and plays his flute, too, so the entire family knows that all is well.

I hiked up the shepherd's hill and sat overlooking the town. On a higher hill, just beyond the simple tin roof of its mosque, I saw the letters G Ü Z E L Y U R T spelled out in rocks. Listening to the timeless sounds of the community, I thought how there are countless Güzelyurts, scattered across every country on earth. Each is humble, yet filled with rich traditions, proud people, and its own village-centric view of our world. Güzelyurt means "beautiful land." While few visitors would consider it particularly beautiful, that's how the people who call it home see it. They'd live nowhere else. And for them, it truly is a *güzel yurt.*

Defending the Separation of Mosque and State...for Now

When visiting eastern Turkey, you don't have a list of sights. It's a cultural scavenger hunt. Years ago, I was exploring with a tour group and we saw 300 kids in a stadium. We dropped in to see what was going on. They were thrusting their fists into the air, screaming in unison, "We are a secular nation! We are a secular nation!" I asked my local guide, "What's going on? Don't they like God?" She said, "Yes, we love God here in Turkey, but—with the rising tide of Islamic fundamentalism just over the border in Iran—we are very concerned about the fragile and precious separation of mosque and state in our country." I was surprised to learn that their hard-won constitution actually requires that the military overthrow the government if it ever becomes a theocracy.

Turkey still is a secular nation. But lately, with each election, the line between mosque and state gets a little more blurred. Turkey, like so much of today's world, is in a tug-of-war between secular forces and right-wing fundamentalism. And, just as in other Islamic lands, Turkish fundamentalist groups use fear of perceived American meddling to win public support. With

People around the world are passionate about their struggles.

the ramped-up economic metabolism that comes with globalization—all those modern changes I found so striking—people whose time-honored ways are threatened cling to what makes their cultures and societies unique. They seek solace in their rituals, religion, and traditions.

My most recent trip happened to coincide with the holy month of Ramadan, when practicing Muslims refrain from eating, drinking, or even smoking during daylight hours. During this time, the Muslim faith seems all the more vivid and engaging. As an oblivious tourist, I kept stumbling into the subtle ways Ramadan affects everyday life. Sucking sweet apple tobacco from a water pipe, I offered my waiter a puff of my hookah. He put his hand over his heart and explained he'd love to, but he couldn't until the sun went down. During Ramadan, if you sleep lightly, you'll wake to the call to prayer and the sounds of a convivial meal just before dawn. As the sun rises, the fast begins. Then, as the sun sets, the food comes out, and the nightly festival begins. Muhammad broke his fast with a dried date or an olive—which remain the most common fast-breakers. Saying, *"Allah kabul etsin"* ("May God accept our fast today"), the staff at a restaurant where I was having only a glass of tea welcomed me to photograph them, and then offered to share their meal.

Anywhere in Islam, witnessing the breaking of the day-long Ramadan fast at sundown is like watching children waiting for the recess bell. Throughout my visit, every time I witnessed this ritual, people offered to share their food. At that restaurant, I said, "No, thanks," but they set me up anyway—with figs, lentil soup, bread, baklava, and Coke. (I thought the Coke was a bit odd… but they said it's not considered American anymore. Coke is truly global.)

Much as I enjoy these Ramadan experiences, my latest visit left me with an uneasy awareness of how fundamentalism is creeping into the mainstream. Mayors now play a part in organizing Ramadan festivities. During Ramadan, no-name neighborhood mosques literally overflow during prayer time. With carpets unfurled on sidewalks, it's a struggle just walking down the street. I got the unsettling feeling that the inconvenience to passing pedestrians wasn't their concern…as if they felt everyone should be praying rather than trying to get somewhere.

I don't want to overstate Turkey's move to the right, but keen and caring secular observers see an ominous trend. I have friends in Turkey almost distraught at their country's slide toward fundamentalism. To them, it's an evolution that—like a rising tide—seems impossible to stop.

Imagine watching your country gradually slip into a theocracy: one universal interpretation of scripture, prayer in school, religious dress codes, women covering up and accepting a scripturally ordained subservient role to men, judges chosen on the basis of the dominant religion, laws and textbooks being rewritten. When the separation of religion and state is violated, a moralistic ruling class that believes they are right and others are wrong sets about reshaping its society.

Seeing this struggle play out in Turkey—a land that first adopted a modern, secular constitution only in 1924—is dramatic. I can feel the chill sweep across a teahouse when a fundamentalist Muslim man walks by…followed, a few steps behind, by his covered-up wife.

For a traveler, the move to the religious right is easiest to see in peoples' clothes. As the father of a teenage girl who did her best to dress trendier than her parents allowed, I am intrigued by teenage Muslim girls covering up under scarves and, I imagine, duress. Sure, they're covered from head to toe. But under their modest robe, you know that many wear chic clothes and high heels.

Throughout Islam, scarves are widely used both as tools for modesty and as fashion accessories. In a fine silk shop, I asked a young woman to demonstrate scarf-wrapping techniques. She happily showed off various demure styles. I asked her to demonstrate how to turn one of her scarves into a conserva-

tive religious statement. It took some convincing before she obliged. She tied the scarf under her chin and around her face, and then, with an extra fold across the forehead, suddenly she became orthodox. The power of that last fold gave me goose bumps. She took it off with a shudder.

Later that day, I dropped by Istanbul's Eyüp Sultan Mosque, where all women wore their scarves with that forehead fold. Famous in Istanbul as the mosque attracting the most conservative worshippers, even its state-employed female security guards were wearing strict, religious headscarves. To my secular Turkish friend, it was striking—even ominous—that state employees would be seen in this garb.

The courtyard outside the mosque was filled with a kind of religious trade fair. Stalls offering free food, literature, and computer programs (with a Mavis Beacon-type prayer guide) stood side by side. Using incentives to target poor and less-educated Turks, it reminded me of the old-school strategy of Christian missionaries. The propaganda seemed mostly directed at women. My friend believes that women, even more than men, are pulling secular Muslim societies like Turkey to the right.

The mosque was filled to capacity, and the courtyard was jammed with the overflow crowd. Women knelt to pray next to their men. But my Turkish friend predicted that in two years, the sexes would be segregated. She pointed to a stairway already filled with fundamentalist women who believed they should worship separately. They've staked out this zone until a formal women's area can be established.

Marketers know that women make the purchasing decisions in American families. Considering this, I ponder whether women make the religious decisions in Turkish families, and to what degree women really are behind the changes in moderate Muslim societies like Turkey. I consider the impact women have on the political discourse in my country. It's interesting that, in both our society and Muslim societies, women with an agenda can be at odds. Some women push their rights in terms of "family values," while others push their agenda in terms of "women's liberation."

Many things drive religious people to get political: a desire for economic justice, a moral environment in which to raise their children, equal rights, the "sanctity of life," and hopes for salvation. These are powerful forces that can easily be manipulated by clever political marketing. They can drive people to war and they know no cultural or political boundaries.

Observing the enthusiasm of this very religious crowd in the courtyard of the mosque, I could imagine someone who had never been outside of the USA dropping in on this scene—and being quite shocked by it all. I asked my Muslim friend, "Should a Christian be threatened by Islam?" She said, "If you have self-confidence in your system, assuming it deserves to survive, it will. Christendom should be threatened by Islam only if the Christian West seeks empire here."

I find an irony in the current tensions between America and Islam. I believe we're incurring incalculable costs (both direct and indirect, tangible and intangible) because our lack of understanding makes us needlessly fearful about Islam. And sadly, I fear that because we're afraid of it, our actions create a situation where we need to be afraid.

Islam in a Pistachio Shell

As our generation sorts through the tensions between Islam and Christendom, a rudimentary understanding of the Muslim faith is a good life skill for any engaged non-Muslim. Here's an admittedly basic and simplistic outline designed to help travelers from the Christian West better understand a complex and often misunderstood culture.

Muslims, like Christians and Jews, are monotheistic. They call God "Allah." The key figure in the Islamic faith is Muhammad, Allah's final and most important prophet, who lived from A.D. 570 to 632. When Muhammad's name appears in print, it's often followed by "PBUH": Peace Be Upon Him.

Just as Christians come in two basic varieties (Protestants and Catholics), Muslims come in two branches. After Muhammad died in A.D. 632, his followers argued over who should succeed him in leading his Islamic faith and state, causing Islam to splinter into two rival factions. Today Shias (a.k.a. "Shiites," less than 15 percent of all Muslims) are concentrated in Iran and Iraq, while Sunnis dominate the rest of the Islamic world (including Turkey and Morocco).

The "five pillars" of Islam are the same for all Muslims. Followers of Islam should:

1. Say and believe, "There is only one God, and Muhammad is his prophet."

2. Pray five times a day, facing Mecca (denoted inside a mosque by a niche called a *mihrab*). Modern Muslims believe that, along with thinking of God, part of the value of this ritual is to help people wash, exercise, and stretch.

3. Give to the poor one-fortieth of your wealth, if you are not in debt. ("Debt" includes the responsibility to provide both your parents and your children with a good life.)

4. Fast during daylight hours through the month of Ramadan. Fasting is about self-discipline. It's also a great social equalizer that helps everyone feel the hunger of the poor.

5. Visit Mecca. Muslims who can afford it and who are physically able are expected to go on a pilgrimage *(Hajj)* to the sacred sites in Mecca and Medina at least once in their lifetime. This is interpreted by some Muslims as a command to travel. My favorite Muhammad quote: "Don't tell me how educated you are; tell me how much you've traveled."

The Islamic equivalent of the Christian bell tower is a minaret, which the *muezzin* traditionally climbs to sing the call to prayer. While traditionally minarets were grand (as pictured here), in a kind of architectural Darwinism, they are shrinking. As calls to prayer are now electronically amplified, the *muezzin* sings into a mic at ground level, and the minaret's height is no longer necessary or worth the expense. Many small, modern mosques have one mini-minaret about as awe-inspiring as your little toe.

Call to Prayer

While the call to prayer sounds spooky to many Americans, I find that with some understanding it becomes beautiful. Traditionally, just before the sun rises, an imam (prayer leader) stares at his arm. When he can tell a gray hair from a black one, it's time to call his community to prayer. While quality and warble varies, across Islam the Arabic words of the call to prayer are exactly the same. The first call to prayer of the day starts with an extra line:

Praying is better than sleeping
God is great (Allahhhhhh hu akbar...)
I witness there is no other God but Allah
I witness Muhammad is Allah's prophet
Come join the prayer
Come to be saved
God is great...God is great
There is no other God but Allah.

Big mosques have a trained professional singer for a *muezzin.* Many tiny mosques can't afford a real *muezzin,* so the imam himself does the call to prayer. The qualitative difference can be obvious. Invariably, my hotel seems to be within earshot of five or six mosques, which creates quite a cacophony.

My challenge is to hear the Muslim call to prayer as a beautiful form of praise that sweeps across the globe—from Malaysia across Pakistan, Arabia, and Turkey to Morocco and then to America—like a stadium wave, undulating exactly as fast as the earth turns...five times a day.

Prayer services in a mosque are usually gender-segregated. The act of praying is quite physical, and—as a practical matter of respect for women (and less distraction for both sexes)—they typically worship apart from the men.

Just as pre-Vatican II Catholicism embraced Latin (for tradition, uniformity, and so all could relate and worship together anywhere, anytime), Islam embraces Arabic. Turks recently experimented by doing the call to prayer in Turkish, but they switched back to the traditional Arabic.

The Quran teaches that Abraham was a good submitter (to the will of God). The word for submitter is "Muslim"—derived from *Islam* ("submit") with a *Mu-* ("one who"). So a Muslim is, literally, "one who submits."

Wherever I travel, having just a basic grasp of the dominant local religion makes the people and traditions I encounter more meaningful and enjoyable. Exploring Muslim countries leaves me with memories of the charming conviviality of neighborhoods spilling into the streets. Like Christmas is a fun time to enjoy the people energy of a Christian culture, Ramadan is a particularly fun and vibrant time to be among Muslims. My visits to places like Turkey, Morocco, and Iran (described in Chapter 8) have shown me how travel takes the fear out of foreign ways.

Morocco: Everything but Pork

Islam is as varied culturally as Christendom. Turkey is unique among Muslim states because it's trying to join the European Union and because of its alliance with the US (important during the Cold War, Gulf War, and Iraq War). Morocco, another Muslim country, offers a different insight into Islam.

On my last visit to Morocco, what I found pleased me: a Muslim nation succeeding, stable, and becoming more affluent with no apparent regard for the US.

Tangier, which I once called "the Tijuana of Africa," used to make me nervous. But the city has changed radically in the last few years…and so has my assessment of it. It was a neglected hellhole for a generation. Tangier was an international city—favored by the West and therefore disdained by Morocco's previous king. He made a point to divert all national investment away from his country's fourth-largest city.

The new king—Mohammed VI, who took the throne in 1999—believes Tangier should be a great city again and has provided the funds to make it happen. The first city he visited after his coronation was Tangier. His support has changed the city and the difference is breathtaking. While Tangier is still exotic—with its dilapidated French colonial and Art Deco buildings giving it a time-warp charm—it's much more efficient, people-friendly, safe-feeling, and generally likable.

Checking into Hotel Continental, I was greeted by flamboyant Jimmy, who runs the shop there. Jimmy knows every telephone area code in the US. A few years ago, I had told him I was from Seattle. He said, "206." Now I tested him again. He said, "206, 360, 425...new area codes."

Hotel Continental had me looking for the English Patient. Gramophones gathered dust on dressers under mangy chandeliers. A serene woman painted a sudsy figure-eight in the loose tiles with her mop, day after day, surrounded by dilapidation that never went away.

As I updated the information in my guidebook, I found a striking and nonchalant incompetence. My guidebook listed the hotel's phone and email data more accurately than their own printed material. It's a 70-room hotel with, it seemed, not a sheet of paper in its office.

Roosters and the Muslim call to prayer worked together to wake me and the rest of that world. When the morning sun was high enough to send a rainbow plunging into the harbor amid ferries busily coming and going, I stood on my balcony and surveyed Tangier kicking into gear. Women in colorful, flowing robes walked to sweatshops adjacent to the port. They were happy to earn $8 a day (a decent wage for an unskilled worker here) sewing for big-name European clothing lines—a reminder that a vast and wealthy Continent is just a short cruise to the north. Cabbies jostled at the pier for the chance to rip off arriving tourists.

Morocco's new king is more modern, and with his friendly policies, Tangier is enjoying a renaissance.

It's an exciting time in Morocco. Walking the streets, I enjoyed observing a modest new affluence, lots of vision and energy, and, at the same time, no compromise with being Arabic and Muslim. The king is modernizing. His queen, a commoner, is the first queen to be seen in public. Moroccans have never seen their king's mother. The fact that Moroccans couldn't even recognize their former queen shows how much can change in a relatively short time.

Women are making gains throughout Moroccan society. Until recently, a woman here couldn't open a bank account. Today the general director of the stock exchange in Casablanca is a woman. Out of 21 ministers voted into office in a recent election, seven are female.

The Moroccans I encountered didn't emulate or even seem to care about the USA. Al-Jazeera blared on teahouse TVs, with stirring images of American atrocities inflicted on fellow Muslims. But people appeared numb to the propaganda, and the TV seemed to be on that channel for lack of an alternative. I felt no animosity directed toward me as an American. There was no political edge to any graffiti or posters.

When I tried to affirm my observations with my guide, Aziz, he explained to me the fundamental difference between "Islamic" and "Islamist": Islamists are expansionist and are threatened by the very existence of Israel. He explained how Al-Jazeera appeals to Islamists. Its reporting is as "fair and balanced" as we'd find on Fox News in the USA. And then Aziz made it clear that Morocco is Islamic, not Islamist.

Wandering in Tangier—especially after dark—is entertaining. It's a rare place where signs are in three languages (Arabic, French, and Spanish)... and English doesn't make the cut. Sometimes, when I'm frustrated with the impact of American foreign policy on the developing world, I have this feeling that an impotent America is better for the world than an America whose power isn't always used for good. Seeing a country where the signs are in three languages, but still ignore English, reminds me that there's a world that's managing just fine without us.

The market scene was a wonderland—of everything but pork: Mountains of glistening olives, a full palate of spices, children with knives happy to perform for my camera.

Aziz explained that each animal is slaughtered in accordance with Islamic law, or Halal. I asked him to explain. He took me to a table with a pile of chickens and hollered "Muhammad!" to catch the attention of a knife-wielding boy. (That confused me until Aziz explained that when he wants someone's attention, he says, "Hey, Muhammad!" It's like our "Hey, you"...but very respectful. For a woman, you'd holler, "Hey, Fatima.") He asked the boy to demonstrate the proper way to slaughter an animal, and I was given a graphic demonstration: in the name of Allah, with a sharp knife, animal's head pointing to Mecca, body drained of its blood.

Before this visit, I had recommended to my guidebook readers that day-trippers from Spain just hold their nose and take the organized tour (with all the big bus groups from Spain's Costa del Sol). A Tangier guide meets you at the ferry. He takes you on a bus tour of the city and a walk through the old town, where he leads you to a few staged photo ops (camel ride, snake charmer, Atlas Mountains tribal musicians). After visiting a clichéd restaurant where you eat clichéd food while a belly dancer performs, you visit a carpet shop. Guides and their tour companies must make a healthy commission.

Why else would they offer the round-trip ferry ride with the tour for the same price as the round-trip ferry ride without the tour?

Being here without a big tour group, I met gracious Moroccans eager to talk and share. About the only time I saw other Westerners was when I crossed

In Morocco, package tourists dine with clichés and each other.

paths with one of the many day-tripping groups. As they completed their visit, these tourists walked in a tight, single-file formation, holding their purses and day bags nervously to their bellies like paranoid kangaroos as they bundled past one last spanking line of street merchants and made it safely back onto the ferry.

I pondered this scene, wondering if these tourists—scared, oblivious, clutching the goodies they traveled so far to pick up on the cheap, and then sailing home without learning a thing—were dealing with Morocco this way because it's the same way their home countries deal with the developing world in general.

It was poignant for me because, until the lessons I learned from this trip, I was part of the problem—recommending the tour rather than the independent adventure. Some of those needlessly paranoid tourists likely had my guidebook in the bag they were clutching. I wished I could grab their books and update all the information that I now realized was bad advice.

While I was comfortable and enjoyed a fascinating Moroccan experience on my own, the frightened tour groups reminded me of some kind of self-inflicted hostage crisis. They sailed away still filled with fear, but I was celebrating an Islamic nation that was stable, enjoying a thriving economy, and that didn't concern itself much with America. The tourists were thankful they didn't get ripped off or diarrhea. I had overcome my fear and was thankful Morocco was doing so well.

In some cases, visiting a country on a tour ruins any opportunity to really learn about that place. While that may be a lost opportunity and a costly mistake, it can also be a valuable lesson. Any one of those tourists could return and, with a different attitude (and better guidebook advice), be welcomed not as a customer, but as a friend.

The Human, the Bear, and the Forest

I am a Christian who wants to believe we can live peacefully with Islam. One thing is clear to me: What I learn about Islam from media in the US can fill me with fear and anger. What I learn about Islam by traveling in Muslim countries fills me with hope.

Of course there are real dangers. And rare is the religion whose fundamentalist fringe wouldn't kill in the name of God. But no society should fear another society simply because their leaders and media say they should. Before anyone hardens their take on Islam, a little travel to a moderate Muslim country can be a good idea. (It's a sad irony that terrorism causes Americans to travel less.) If you can't visit in person, travel to Islam vicariously by seeking out connections and friendships with people from cultures and religions that are different from your own.

The centuries-old tension between Christendom and Islam is like a human sharing a forest with a bear. Both just want to gather berries, do a little fishing, raise their kids, and enjoy the sun. Neither wants to do harm to the other, but—because they can't readily communicate—either would likely kill the other if they crossed paths. The world is our forest and we're sharing it with others. As it gets smaller, more and more cultures will cross paths. Our advantage over the human and the bear: we can communicate.

Chapter 7
Europe: Not "Hard on Drugs" or "Soft on Drugs"...but Smart on Drugs

Because of my travels, I find myself one of the most high-profile people in the country advocating the reform of our nation's marijuana laws. I've produced a TV show on the topic with the ACLU, and have been a board member of NORML, the National Organization for the Reform of Marijuana Laws, since 2003. But I am certainly not "pro-drugs." I simply appreciate how most of Europe treats its drug problems in a pragmatic way, with success measured by harm reduction rather than incarceration. While in the US 80,000 people are in jail for marijuana charges, in parts of Europe discreetly smoking a joint is just another form of relaxation.

I speak out on this issue, in part, because most Americans cannot—out of fear of losing their job or reputation or both. Of the countless good causes I could get involved in, drug policy reform is a high-risk choice. When I'm interviewed about this on TV or radio, journalists ask me all the predictable questions...and then, as soon as the mic is off, they say, "Thanks for having the courage to speak out." My first thought is that if it seems courageous to challenge a law one believes is wrong, that is, in itself, reason to speak out. Since I own my own business, I can't get fired... and so, when it comes to America's prohibition on marijuana, I can consider lessons learned from my travels and say what I really believe when I'm back home.

The US and Europe: Two Different Approaches to Drug Abuse

There's no doubt that the abuse of drugs—whether "soft drugs" (such as marijuana, alcohol, and tobacco) or "hard drugs" (including heroin, cocaine, and methamphetamines)—is horrible and destroys lives. Since the 1970s, the US's approach has been (with the exception of alcohol and tobacco) to declare a "war on drugs." In contrast, Europe has attempted a wide range of solutions to the same problem. And, while Europe certainly doesn't have all the answers, their results have been compelling. I've traveled with an appetite for learning why Europe has fewer drug-related deaths, less drug-related incarceration, and less drug consumption per capita than we do here in America. (I have to admit, though, that as I reviewed the numbers to back up my claims for this chapter, I discovered one irrefutable fact: Statistics on drug use and abuse are all over the map. While most of the empirical studies reinforce my conclusions, conflicting data always seem to emerge. I assume this is because most sources have an agenda—pro or con—which skews their findings.)

To be clear, there is no Europe-wide agreement on drug policy. Some countries—including the Netherlands, Spain, Portugal, and Switzerland—categorize marijuana as a soft drug (similar to alcohol and tobacco). Others—including Sweden and Greece—strictly enforce laws against both marijuana and hard drugs (in fact, drug-related arrests are on the rise in some countries). But what most European countries have in common is an emphasis on education and prevention. They believe that by handling drug abuse more as a public health problem than as a criminal one, they are better able to reduce the harm it causes—both to the individual (health problems and antisocial behavior) and to society (healthcare costs, policing costs, and drug-related crime).

In an Amsterdam "coffeeshop," you won't find coffee.

Generally, Europeans employ a three-pronged strategy for dealing with hard drugs: law enforcement, education, and healthcare. Police zero in on dealers—not users—to limit the supply of drugs. Users generally get off with a warning and are directed to get treatment; any legal action respects the principle of proportionality. Anti-drug education programs work hard to warn people (particularly teenagers) of the dangers of drugs. And finally, the medical community steps in to battle health problems associated with drug use (especially HIV/AIDS and hepatitis C) and to help addicts reclaim their lives.

When it comes to soft drugs, policies in much of Europe are also more creative and pragmatic than America's. We'll get into an illuminating case study (the Netherlands) later in this chapter.

I'm not saying Europe always gets it right. They have employed some silly tactics in efforts to curb marijuana use. For example, a study in France showed that boys smoke more pot than girls, which they attributed to boys being nervous about approaching girls socially. So they literally gave boys government-funded training in flirting. While this notion seems ridiculous, you have to admit it's refreshing to see legislators thinking "outside the box." Even if some of their ideas fail, others turn out to be brilliant.

Meanwhile, the US seems afraid to grapple with this problem openly and creatively. Rather than acting as a deterrent, the US criminalization of marijuana drains precious resources, clogs our legal system, and distracts law enforcement attention from more pressing safety concerns. Of the many billions of tax dollars we invest annually fighting our war on drugs, more than two-thirds is spent on police, courts, and prisons. On the other hand, European nations—seeking a cure that isn't more costly than the problem itself—spend a much larger portion of their drug policy funds on doctors, counselors, and clinics. According to the EU website, European policymakers estimate that they save 15 euros in police and healthcare costs for each euro invested in drug education, addiction prevention, and counseling.

Like Europe, the US should be open to new solutions. It's out of character for a nation so famous for its ingenuity to simply label the drug problem a "war" and bring in the artillery. Europeans make a strong case that approaching drug abuse from the perspective of harm reduction can be very effective.

And so, to find inspiration, let's take a closer look at how two European countries deal with drug use: the famously tolerant Dutch stance on the soft drug of marijuana, and the pragmatic Swiss approach to the hard drug of heroin.

The Dutch Approach to Marijuana

Amsterdam, Europe's counterculture mecca, thinks the concept of a "victimless crime" is a contradiction in terms. The city—and all of the Netherlands—is famous for its progressive attitude about marijuana. Regardless of your views, it's fascinating to try to understand the Dutch system that, in 1976, decriminalized the personal recreational use of pot. I travel to Amsterdam frequently, and on each visit, as a part of my guidebook research chores, I talk to various locals about marijuana—from the guys who run shops that sell pot, to pot-smokers and non-smokers, to police officers who deal with drug problems face-to-face. Here's what I've learned.

First off, marijuana is not actually "legal" in the Netherlands—Dutch law still technically defines marijuana use as a crime (any country experimenting with treating drugs as a healthcare rather than a criminal issue knows it risks costly trade sanctions from the US). But for more than 30 years, the nation's prosecutors have made it a policy not to enforce that law under their guiding principle of expediency: It makes no sense to enforce a law that is more trouble than it's worth.

The Dutch are justly famous for their practice of *gedogen*—toleration. They believe that as soon as you criminalize something, you lose any ability to regulate it. So they tolerate recreational pot smoking in order to regulate it (the same way we tolerate and regulate alcohol and tobacco). But Dutch tolerance has its limits. The moment you hurt or threaten someone else, the crime is no longer victimless—and no longer tolerated. Dutch laws against driving under the influence—whether alcohol or marijuana—are extremely tough.

Throughout the Netherlands, you'll see "coffeeshops": pubs selling marijuana. The minimum age for purchase is 18, and coffeeshops can sell up to five grams of marijuana per person per day. As long as you're a paying customer (for instance, you

In a Dutch coffeeshop, the menu features service with a smile—but no coffee.

buy a drink), you can pop into any coffeeshop and light up, even if you didn't buy your pot there.

Because of laws prohibiting the advertising of marijuana, the customer generally must take the initiative to get the menu. Locals buy marijuana by asking, "Can I see the cannabis menu?" In some places, there's a button you have to push and hold down to illuminate the otherwise-invisible list of creatively named strains of pot and hash.

The Netherlands' recent ban on public smoking (designed to protect workers from their customers' secondhand smoke) pertains to tobacco smoke, but not pot smoke. This matters in coffeeshops because Europeans generally mix their marijuana with tobacco. It might seem strange to an American, but if a Dutch coffeeshop is busted... it's because of tobacco. Shops have developed a kind of "herbal tea" mix as a tobacco substitute for joints. Coffeeshops with a few outdoor seats have a huge advantage, as their customers who prefer joints with a tobacco/marijuana mix can legally light up outside. But shops without the outdoor option have struggled.

Essentially legal since 1976, an impressive variety of marijuana joints fills the sales racks in Dutch coffeeshops.

Because pot is retailed much like beer or cigarettes, varieties evolve with demand. Several forms of the cannabis plant are sold. Locals smoke the pressed resin of the cannabis plant (hashish) and the buds and leaf of the plant (marijuana or grass). While each shop has different brands, all marijuana is either Indica or Sativa. Indica gets you a "stony, heavy, mellow, couch weed" high. Sativa is light, fun, uplifting, and more psychedelic—it makes you giggle.

Most of the marijuana you'll see these days is local. Growing technology has improved (allowing for more exotic local strains), and it's much safer to deal with Dutch plants than import marijuana from faraway lands. (International trafficking is a whole different legal complexity than growing and selling your own domestic strain.)

Pre-rolled joints are sold in three ways: pure; with the non-tobacco "hamburger helper" herbal mix; or rolled with tobacco. (Pure marijuana joints are easier to find now than before the ban on tobacco smoking.) Some shops sell individual joints (averaging about $4 each). Others sell only small packs of three or four joints.

Shops also sell marijuana and hash in little baggies, which usually cost $15 to $20. Shops have loaner bongs and new-fangled inhalers for the health nuts. They dispense cigarette papers like toothpicks. Some shops sell bags in uniform weights, others in uniform prices. I'm told the better pot, with a higher price tag, is not necessarily more expensive—as it takes less to get high and gives you a better high.

Locals warn Americans—unaccustomed to the strength of the local stuff—to try a lighter leaf. In fact, they are generally very patient in explaining the varieties available. American tourists, giddy at the chance to smoke in public without the paranoia that comes with smoking back home, are notorious for overdoing it. When they call an ambulance, medics just say, unsympathetically, "Drink something sweet and walk it off."

The tax authorities don't want to see more than 500 grams (about a pound) on the books at the end of each accounting cycle. Being caught with too much inventory is one of the more common ways shops lose their license. A shop could retail a ton of pot with no problem, as long as it maintains that tiny stock and refills it as needed. This law is designed to keep shops small and prevent them from becoming bases for exportation—which would bring more international pressure on the Netherlands to crack down on its coffeeshop culture. (Amsterdam's mayor—understanding that this regulation just has the city busy with small-time deliveries—has proposed doubling the allowable inventory level to a kilo. Just the thought of a big city mayor grappling with a practical issue like this so pragmatically is striking.)

The wholesale dimension of the marijuana business is the famous "gray area" in the law. Rather than deal with that complex issue, Dutch lawmakers just left wholesaling out of the equation, taking the "don't ask, don't tell" route. Most shops get their inventory from the pot equivalent of home brewers or microbrewers. Shops with better "boutique suppliers" get the reputation for having better-quality weed (and regularly win the annual Cannabis Cup trophy).

Everyone I've talked with in Amsterdam agrees that pot should never be bought on the street. Well-established coffeeshops are considered much safer, as their owners have an incentive to keep their trade safe and healthy.

The Prohibition of Our Age

Travel teaches us a respect for history. And when it comes to drug policy, I hope we can learn from our own prohibitionist past. Back in the 1920s, America's biggest drug problem was alcohol. To combat it, we made booze illegal and instituted Prohibition. By any sober assessment, all that Prohibition produced was grief. By criminalizing a soft drug that people refused to stop enjoying, Prohibition created the mob (Al Capone and company), filled our prisons, and cost our society a lot of money. It was big government at its worst. Finally, courageous citizens stood up and said the laws against alcohol were causing more problems than the alcohol itself. When Prohibition was repealed in 1933, nobody was saying "booze is good." Society just realized that the laws were counterproductive and impossible to enforce. In our own age, many lawyers, police officers, judges, and other concerned citizens are coming to the same conclusion about the current US government-sponsored prohibition against marijuana.

At Seattle's annual Hempfest, 80,000 people call for an end to America's prohibition on marijuana. On the main stage, I talk up Europe's more pragmatic approach to drug abuse.

The Dutch are not necessarily "pro-marijuana." In fact, most have never tried it or even set foot in a coffeeshop. They just don't think the state has any business preventing the people who want it from getting it in a sensible way. To appease Dutch people who aren't comfortable with marijuana, an integral component of the coffeeshop system is discretion. It's bad form to smoke marijuana openly while walking down the street. Dutch people who don't like pot don't have to encounter or even smell it. And towns that don't want coffeeshops don't have them. Occasionally a coffeeshop license will not be renewed in a particular neighborhood, as the city wants to keep a broad smattering of shops (away from schools) rather than a big concentration in any one area.

Statistics support the Dutch belief that their more pragmatic system removes crime from the equation without unduly increasing consumption: After 30 years of handling marijuana this way, Dutch experts in the field of drug-abuse prevention agree that, while marijuana use has increased slightly, it has not increased more than in other European countries where pot-smokers are being arrested. (According to a 2005 study, 23 percent of Dutch people have used pot, compared to 23 percent of Germans and 30 percent of French.) And for you nervous parents: The Dutch have seen no significant change in marijuana consumption among teens (who, according to both US and EU government statistics, smoke pot at half the US rate). Meanwhile, in the US, many teens report that it's easier for them to buy marijuana than tobacco or alcohol—because they don't get carded when buying something illegally.

It's interesting to compare European use to the situation back home, where marijuana laws are strictly enforced. According to *Forbes Magazine*, 25 million Americans currently use marijuana (federal statistics indicate that one in three Americans has used marijuana at some point), which makes it a $113 billion untaxed industry in our country. The FBI reports that about 40 percent of the roughly 1.8 million annual drug arrests in the US are for marijuana—the vast majority (89 percent) for simple possession...that means users, not dealers.

Many Dutch people believe that their pot policies have also contributed to the fact that they have fewer hard drug problems than other countries. The thinking goes like this: A certain segment of the population will experiment with drugs regardless. The coffeeshop scene allows people to do this safely, with soft drugs. Police see the coffeeshops as a firewall separating soft drug use from hard drug abuse in their communities. If there is a dangerous chemical being pushed on the streets, for example, the police (with the help of coffeeshop proprietors) communicate to the drug-taking part of their society via the coffeeshops. When considering the so-called "gateway" effect of marijuana, the only change the police have seen in local heroin use is that the average age of a Dutch needle addict is getting older. In fact, the Dutch believe marijuana only acts as a "gateway" drug when it is illegal—because then, young people have no option but to buy it from pushers on the street, who have an economic incentive to get them hooked on more expensive and addictive hard drugs.

The hope and hunch is that people go through their drug-experimentation phase innocently with pot, and then the vast majority move on in life without getting sucked into harder, more dangerous drugs. Again, the numbers bear this out: Surveys show that more than three times as many Americans (1.4%) report having tried heroin as Dutch people (0.4%).

Studying how the Dutch retail marijuana is interesting. It's also helpful because learning how another society confronts a persistent problem differently than we do can help us envision how we might deal with the same problem more effectively. I agree with my Dutch friends, who remind me that a society has to make a choice: tolerate alternative lifestyles...or build more prisons. The Netherlands has made its choice. We're still building more prisons. (My Dutch friends needle me with the fact that only the US and Russia lock up more than one percent of their citizens, while the average per capita incarceration rate in Europe is only a tenth the US rate.) I also agree with New York Mayor LaGuardia. Way back in the 1930s, when it was becoming clear that America's Prohibition on alcohol wasn't working, LaGuardia said that if a society has a law on the books that it doesn't intend to enforce consistently, it erodes respect for all laws in general.

While the Dutch are famously lenient in their marijuana laws, many other European countries are also progressive on this issue. I've chatted with people passing a joint as they played backgammon in the shadow of the cathedral in Bern. They told me that marijuana enforcement is stricter in Switzerland each spring at the start of the travel season, so the country doesn't become a magnet for the backpacking pot-smoker crowd (an admitted drawback to the Dutch system). And I've talked with twentysomethings in Copenhagen rolling a joint on the steps of their city hall, who say they have to be a little careful because the Danes are required to arrest a couple of pot-smokers each year in order to maintain favored trade status with the US.

The Swiss Approach to Hard Drugs

Marijuana is one thing. But hard drugs—such as heroin—are another. And, even as some European countries are liberalizing their approach to pot, they draw a clear distinction between "soft" and "hard" drugs. Hard drug abuse—with an estimated two million problem users—is a concern in Europe, just as it is in the US. There is no easy solution. But the pragmatic European approach—based on harm reduction rather than punishment for an immoral act—appears to have had some success. Switzerland has been at the forefront of these efforts.

If you don't want junkies shooting up in your toilet, just install blue lights.

The last time I was in Switzerland, I dropped into a Starbucks in down-town Zürich, went downstairs into the bathroom...and it was all blue. I had stumbled into another example of a creative European drug policy. The Swiss, who don't want their junkies shooting up in public bathrooms, install blue lights. I couldn't see my veins...you couldn't shoot up if you wanted to.

Of course, this minor frustration wouldn't stop junkies from finding a fix. Across the street is a machine that once sold cigarettes. Now it sells hygienic, government-subsidized syringes—three for two francs, less than a buck apiece. The Swiss recognize that heroin doesn't spread HIV/AIDS or other deadly diseases. Dirty needles do. If addicts need more than just sterile needles, they know they can go down the street to a heroin-maintenance clinic for their fix. Rather than steal (or worse) to finance their addiction, they get the services of a nurse and a counselor. Swiss society is working to help addicts stay alive, get off of welfare, and rejoin the workforce. Clinic workers told me that in Switzerland, crime and AIDS cases related to heroin use have decreased, while recovery and employment rates among their clients have increased.

When addicts aren't nervous about where they'll get their next fix, con-sumption goes down (as do overdoses). When demand on the streets goes down, so does the price. This brings down street violence...and is bad news for a pusher's bottom line. With clean needles and a source providing reliable purity, potency, and quantity, maintaining the addiction becomes less dangerous. With these provisions, you still have an addict—but you remove crime, violence, money, and disease from the equation, so you can treat it for what it is: a health problem for mixed-up people who are screwing up their lives and need help. As Swiss addicts are safely dosed to maintenance levels, they begin to reclaim their lives, get jobs, pay taxes, and—in many cases—kick their habit altogether. Switzerland's heroin maintenance centers (now also in Germany and the Nether-lands) succeed in reducing the harm caused by drug abuse.

Swiss machines that once sold cigarettes now sell government-subsidized syringes. When it comes to needles in Switzerland, no one shares.

While heroin-maintenance programs have been relatively

successful, Europeans have tried and failed with other programs. For instance, experimental "needle parks" (places where the hard drug-taking community could gather) ended up attracting junkies and creating a public nuisance. These were abandoned for the more low-key maintenance centers. But at least Europeans are dealing with the challenge openly, creatively, and compassionately.

Dutch cops, happy to ignore pot smokers since 1976 (but still tough on hard drugs), measure the effectiveness of their society's drug policy in terms of harm reduction.

In contrast, some observers suggest that the US's more punitive policies towards addicts cause "junkification": they marginalize addicts and drive them to dangerous, predatory behaviors—from simple stealing, to mugging, to prostitution, to selling drugs to others. In other words, if you treat heroin addicts like they're dangerous junkies...that's exactly what they'll become.

The casual American observer who sees more junkies on the streets of Europe than in the US may conclude they have a bigger drug problem because of their more lenient drug policies. In fact, according to the 2007 UN World Drug Report, the percentage of Europeans who use illicit drugs is about half that of Americans. The difference is that theirs are out and about while working with these centers and trying to get their lives back on track. Ours are more often either dead or in jail. Through its busy maintenance centers, Switzerland has provided literally millions of heroin fixes, and they've not had a single overdose death. Overall the US loses roughly 18,000 people a year to hard drug overdoses, and Europe (with a much larger population) loses about 8,000.

Like my European friends, I believe we can adopt a pragmatic policy toward both marijuana and hard drugs, with a focus on harm reduction and public health, rather than tough-talking but counterproductive criminalization. It's time to have an honest discussion about our drug laws and their effectiveness. When it comes to drug policy, you can be soft, hard...or smart.

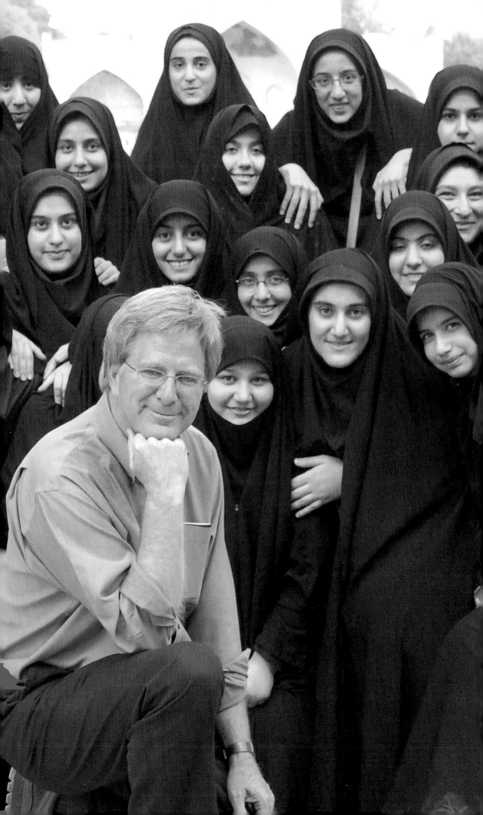

Chapter 8
Mission: Understand Iran

n early 2008, a friend from the Washington State chapter of the United Nations Association called me and asked what I could do to help them build understanding between Iran and the US, and defuse the tension that could lead to war. I answered, "The only thing of any consequence I could do would be to produce a TV show on Iran." Over the next few months, I wrote a proposal for a public television show—no politics, just travel. The title was Iran: Yesterday and Today.

When this project began, like most Americans, I knew next to nothing about Iran. It was a journey of discovery…all caught on film. My hope was to enjoy a rich and fascinating culture, to get to know a nation that's a leader in its corner of the world (and has been for 2,500 years), and to better understand the 70 million people who call Iran home.

I'm convinced that people-to-people travel experiences can be a powerful force for peace. People traveling to the Soviet Union helped us get through the Cold War without things turning hot. Travel to Vietnam has helped heal wounds left in the aftermath of that war. And, as the USA and Iran continue their dangerous flirtation with an avoidable war, travel there can help build understanding between our nations.

Knowing that many Americans won't likely actually travel to Iran, I took my TV crew there to bring the travel experience home to America. Rather than focus on Iran's well-documented offenses—their alleged funding of terrorists, threats to Israel, or nuclear ambitions—I simply wanted to better understand Iran's people and its culture in the hopes that we can sort out our serious differences peacefully and more smartly. While it's common practice for a nation to dehumanize its enemy in a prelude to war, I believe if you're going to bomb someone, you should know them first. It should hurt when you kill someone. My Iran mission turned out to be not only an exciting and enjoyable travel experience, but one of the most gratifying projects I've ever taken on. In addition to addressing some of the deep rifts between our two societies, this chapter also offers a behind-the-scenes peek at traveling and filming in this mysterious country.

The Pilot Said, "We're Taking this Plane to Tehran"...
and Nobody Was Alarmed

Flying from Istanbul's Atatürk Airport to Tehran's Khomeini Airport, I thought about other airports my fellow passengers likely used—Reagan and De Gaulle. The airports are named after four very different 20th-century leaders, but each one left an indelible mark on his nation.

The plane was filled with well-off Iranian people. Their features were different from mine, but they dressed and acted just like me. As so often happens when I travel, I was struck by how people—regardless of the shapes of their

noses—are so similar the world over. As we all settled into the wide-body jet, I wished the big decision-makers of our world weren't shielded from an opportunity to share an economy cabin with people like this.

I had made a similar Istanbul-to-Tehran trip 30 years before. Last time it took three days on a bus, and the Shah was on his last legs. Wandering through Iranian towns in 1978, I remember riot squads in the streets and the Shah's portrait seeming to hang tenuously in market stalls. I also remember

Suddenly it occurs to our producer, Simon, that the plane is filled with Iranians...and everyone has been given a metal knife.

being struck by the harsh gap between rich and poor in Tehran. I was 23 years old and confronted with realities that my friends who stayed home were oblivious to. I believe that was the first time in my life I was angered by economic injustice.

My Istanbul-Tehran trip was quicker this time—three hours rather than three days. And every main square and street that had been named "Shah" back then was now named "Khomeini." On my 1978 visit, all denominations of paper money had one face on them. In 2008, they still did...but the face was different.

As the pilot began our descent, rich and elegant Persian women put on their scarves as routinely as buckling their seatbelts. With all that hair suddenly covered, I noticed how striking long hair can be—how it really does grab a man's attention. Looking out the window into the night, the lights of

Tehran's millions of inhabitants seemed to stretch forever. Greater Tehran has more people than all of Greece (where I woke up that morning).

I thought of the unlikely path that had led me to this point. The permissions had been so slow in coming that the project only became a certainty about a week before the shoot. Because the US does not maintain a diplomatic relationship with Iran, the only way we could communicate was indirectly, via the Iranian Interest Section at the Pakistani Embassy. It was strange to go into a relaxed, almost no-security Iranian Embassy in Athens...and walk out with visas.

Why was Iran letting us in? They actually want to boost Western tourism. I would think this might frighten the Iranian government, since tourists could bring in unwanted ideas (like those that prompted the USSR to restrict tourism). But Iran wants more visitors nonetheless. They also believe that the Western media have made their culture look menacing, and never show its warm, human, and gracious side. They did lots of background research on me and my work, and apparently concluded that my motives were acceptable. They said that, while they'd had problems with other American network crews, they'd had good experiences with PBS film crews.

Not that we were planning to glorify Iran. While I was excited to learn about the rich tapestry of Iranian culture and history, I also recognized that

I couldn't ignore some of the fundamental cultural differences. I felt a responsibility to show the reality women face in Iran, and to try to understand why Iranians always seem to be chanting "Death to America." We wanted to be free-spirited and probing, but not abuse the trust of the Iranian government.

Our "welcome" included building-sized anti-US murals showing American flags with stars of skulls and dropping bombs painting the stripes.

As the plane touched down, I felt a wince of anxiety. This was a strange land for me—and therefore frightening. We had considered leaving our big camera in Greece and just taking the small one. Nervous even about the availability of electricity, I had made sure all my electrical stuff was charged up before leaving Greece. And there were questions: How free would we actually be? Would the hotel rooms be bugged? Was there really absolutely no alcohol—even in fancy hotels? Would crowds gather around us, and then suddenly turn angry?

I was about to set foot in what just might be the most surprising and fascinating land I've ever visited.

Tehran: Iran's Mile-High Metropolis

By my first night in Tehran, it was already clear that Iran was an intriguing and complex paradox: playful Revolutionary Guards, four-lane highways intersecting with no traffic lights, "Death to America" murals, and big, warm, welcoming smiles.

Tehran, a youthful and noisy capital city, is the modern heart of this country. It's a smoggy, mile-high metropolis. With a teeming population of 14 million in the metropolitan area, its apartment blocks stretch far into the surrounding mountains.

I stepped out onto the 15th-floor balcony of my fancy hotel room to hear the hum of the city. I enjoyed the view of a vast, twinkling city at twilight. Fresh snow capped the mountains above the ritzy high-rise condos of North Tehran.

As I looked straight down, I noticed the hotel's entryway buzzing with activity, as it was hosting a conference on Islamic unity. The circular driveway was lined by the flags of 30 nations. Huge collections of flags seemed to be common in Iran—perhaps because it provided a handy opportunity to exclude the Stars and Stripes. (The only American flags I saw during the trip were the ones featured in hateful political murals.)

A van with an X-ray security checkpoint was permanently parked outside the entrance, carefully examining the bags of each visitor. It was interesting to see that Iran, a country we feel we need to protect ourselves from, had its own security headaches.

Back in my room, I nursed a tall glass of pomegranate juice. My lips were puckered from munching lemony pistachios from an elegantly woven tray— the best I've ever tasted (and I am a pistachio connoisseur). I cruised the channels on my TV: CNN, BBC, and—rather than shopping channels—lots of programming designed to set the mood for prayer. One channel showed a mesmerizing river with water washing lovingly over shiny rocks. Another featured the sun setting on Mecca, with live coverage of the pilgrim action at the Kaaba. I was a long way from home...and ready to explore.

Jumping Through Hoops in a Society on Valium

The nuts and bolts of filming in Iran were challenging. Our 12-day Iran shoot included Tehran, Esfahan, Shiraz, and Persepolis. I traveled with my typical skeleton crew of three: Simon Griffith (director), Karel Bauer (cameraman), and me. We also had the help of two Iranian guides: One was an Iranian-American friend who lives in Seattle. The other was appointed by the Iranian government to be with us at all times. This combination was interesting...and tricky.

Traveling through Iran as a film crew presented us with some unique hurdles. On the first day, we dropped by the foreign press office to get our press badges. A beautiful and properly covered woman took mug shots for our badges and carefully confirmed the pronunciation of our names in order to transliterate them into Farsi.

The travel agency—overseen by the "Ministry of Islamic Guidance"— assigned us what they called a "guide," but what I'd call a "government minder." Our guide/minder, Seyed, was required to follow our big camera wherever it went—even if that meant climbing on the back of a motorcycle taxi to

Our guide Seyed was expected to follow our camera at all times. Hang on tight and follow that taxi!

follow our cameraman as he filmed a "point-of-view" shot through wild traffic. When he wasn't holding on for dear life, Seyed slipped a tiny camera out of his pocket and documented our shoot by filming us as we filmed Iran.

While this sounds constraining, Seye proved to be a big help to our production. Whenever we filmed a place of commercial or religious importance, a plainclothes security guard would appear. Then we'd wait around while Seyed explained who we were and what we were doing. No single authority was in charge—many arms of government overlapped and made rules that conflicted with each other. Seyed made our filming possible...or told us when it wasn't.

Routinely I'd look up from my note-taking and see Iranians gathered, curious, and wanting to talk.

Permission to film somewhere was limited to a specific time window. Even if we were allowed to film a certain building on a given day, it didn't mean we could shoot it on a different day, or from the balcony of an adjacent tea house (where we didn't have permission), or from an angle, for instance, that showed a bank (since banks cannot be filmed).

My critics back home skeptically predicted that our access would be very limited—to only the prettiest sights. (Meanwhile, Iranians I met were convinced that I'd doctor our footage to make Iran look ugly and dangerous.) In reality, it was far less restrictive than we'd expected. Some subjects were forbidden for reasons of security (banks, government, military) or modesty ("un-veiled" women). But because we weren't filming an "exposé," we were allowed to shoot all that we needed to—including some provocative subjects, such as anti-American or anti-Israeli murals (more on these later).

We were free to talk to and film people on the street, but this was a bit difficult. When our camera was rolling, it reminded me of my early trips to the USSR, when only those with nothing to lose would risk talking openly. At other times, such as when the crew was busy setting up a shot, I was free to roam about on my own and have fun connecting with locals. (I found that young, educated Iranians spoke English.) I have never traveled to a place where I had such an easy and enjoyable time connecting with people. Locals were as confused and fascinated by me as I was by them.

Bombast and the Axis of Evil

Even from the first moments of this trip, it was clear that the people of Iran would be the biggest joy of our visit. Iranians consider visitors to be a gift from God…and treat them that way.

People greeted me with a smile. Invariably, they asked where I was from. I often said, "You tell me." They guessed and guessed, running through five or six countries before giving up. When I finally told them, "America," they'd be momentarily shocked. They seemed to be thinking, "I thought Americans hate us. Why would one be here like this?" The smile left their face. Then a bigger smile came back as they said, "Welcome!" or "I love America!"

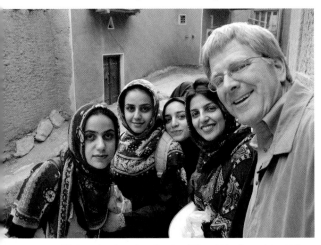

Welcoming travelers is a traditional Muslim value…and being an American makes you the most popular kid in the village.

In a hundred such interactions in our 12 days in Iran, never once did my saying "I am an American" result in anything less than a smile or a kind of "Ohhh, you are rich and strong," or "People and people together no problem, but I don't like your Mr. Bush." (It seemed that Iranians liked our president as much as Americans liked Iran's.) I found it ironic that during the Bush years, Americans found they were better off keeping a low profile in most foreign countries. But in a country I was told hated me, my nationality was a real plus absolutely everywhere I went.

The disparity between the warm welcome I received and the "Axis of Evil" and "Death to America" bickering of our two governments got me thinking about bombast and history.

The word "axis" conjures up images of the alliance of Hitler, Mussolini, and Hirohito that our fathers and grandfathers fought in World War II. People in these countries now believe that each of these leaders maintained his power with the help of his ability to stir the simplistic side of his electorate with bombast.

Today, bombast still hogs the headlines, skewing understanding between the mainstream of each country. For example, Iran's President Mahmoud Ahmadinejad has a kind of Hugo Chavez notoriety around the West for his wild and provocative statements and actions: calling for Israel to be "wiped off the map," denying the existence of the Holocaust, insisting on Iran's right to nuclear arms, and persecuting gay people in Iran. Ahmadinejad is an ideologue, and Americans who find him outrageous are fully justified.

But, much as we might viscerally disagree with Ahmadinejad, it's dangerous to simply dismiss him as a madman. To him, and to his followers, his logic does make sense: If Germany killed the Jews, why are Palestinians (rather than Germans) being displaced to house the survivors? Everyone in Iran understands—better, perhaps, than we foreigners—that Ahmadinejad is more extreme than the Supreme Leader, Ayatollah Ali Khamenei. And, crucially, the Supreme Leader is more powerful than the president. Many locals I talked with discounted Ahmadinejad's most outrageous claims as overstatements intended to shore up his political base. While that doesn't justify the hateful images and slogans I couldn't avoid as I explored his country, it might help explain them.

Meanwhile, Iranians get just as fired up about the rhetoric of American politicians. During our visit (in the summer of 2008), Iranians were still buzzing about the potential presidencies of John McCain (who jokingly rewrote the lyrics of the Beach Boys classic song, "Barbara Ann," to become "bomb bomb bomb, bomb bomb Iran") or Hillary Clinton (who said she would "obliterate" Iran if it attacked Israel). For Iranians, hearing high-profile representatives of the world's lone superpower talk this way was terrifying. Unfortunately, that fear enables people like Ahmadinejad to demonize America in order to stay in power.

Like our children start each school day pledging "allegiance to one nation, under God," Iranian kids are taught their nation's values. Rather than

Iranian government propaganda depicts the US and Israel as sinister partners in a quest for global domination.

Most Iranians genuinely like Americans.

marketing products to consume, billboards sell an ideology. Some are uplifting (Shia scripture reminding people there is wisdom in compassion). Many others glorify heroes who died as martyrs, taunt the US, cheer for Hezbollah, trumpet "Death to America" and "Death to Israel," and so on. These murals mix fear, religion, patriotism, and a heritage of dealing with foreign intervention.

Many things I experienced in Iran fit the negative image that I'd seen back home. But the more I traveled there, the more apparent it became that the standard, media-created image of Iran in the USA was not the whole story. I simply couldn't reconcile the fear-mongering and hate-filled billboards with the huge smiles and genuine hospitality we received on the ground.

Ask anyone who has lived in a country where they disagree with the leaders: Attention-grabbing bombast does not necessarily reflect the feelings of the man or woman on the street. Throughout my visit, I kept thinking: Politicians come and go. The people are here to stay.

Death to...Whatever!

Traffic is notorious in Tehran. Drivers may seem crazy, but I was impressed by their expertise at keeping things moving. At some major intersections, there were no lights—eight lanes would come together at right angles, and everyone just shuffled through. People are great drivers, and, somehow, it works. (It inspired me to drive more aggressively when I got home.)

While the traffic is hair-raising, it's not noisy. Because of a history of motorcycle bandits and assassinations, only smaller, less powerful (and therefore quieter) motorcycles are allowed. To get somewhere in a hurry, motorcycle taxis are a blessing. While most Iranians ignore helmet laws, I was more cautious. I was warned, "It's better to leave a little paint on passing buses than a piece of scalp."

Adding to the chaotic traffic mix are pedestrians, doing their best to navigate the wild streets. Locals joke that when you set out to cross a big street, you "go to Chechnya." I was told that Iran loses more than 30,000 people on the roads each year (in cars and on foot).

While in Tehran, we were zipped smoothly around by Majid, our driver. Majid navigated our eight-seater bus like a motor scooter, weaving in and out of traffic that stayed in its lanes like rocks in a landslide. To illustrate how clueless I was in Iran, for three days I called him "Najaf." And whenever a bit of filming went well and we triumphantly returned to the car, I gave him an enthusiastic thumbs-up. But finally Majid patiently explained that I'd been confusing his name with a city in Iraq...and that giving someone a thumbs-up in Iran is like giving them the finger.

While traffic is enough to make you scream, people are incredibly good-humored on the road. I never heard angry horns honking. While stalled in a Tehran jam, people in a neighboring car saw me sitting patiently in the back of our van: a foreigner stuck in their traffic. They rolled down their window and handed Majid a bouquet of flowers, saying, "Give this to your visitor and apologize for our traffic." When the traffic jam broke up, we moved on—with a bouquet from strangers on my lap.

But traffic can be aggravating, too. Later, as we struggled to drive along a horribly congested street, Majid suddenly declared, "Death to traffic." This outburst caught my attention. I said, "I thought it was 'Death to America.'" He explained, "Here in Iran, when something frustrates us and we have no control over it, this is what we say. 'Death to traffic. Death to...whatever.'"

Cars merge through major intersections without traffic lights as if that's the norm. Surprisingly...it works.

The casual tone of Majid's telling aside made me think differently about one of the biggest concerns many Americans have about Iranians: Their penchant for declaring "Death to" this and that. Did Majid literally want to kill all those drivers that were in our way?

The experience made me wonder if Iranians' "Death to" curses are not so different from Westerners who exclaim, "Damn those French" or "Damn this traffic jam." If we say, "Damn those teenagers," do we really want them to die and burn in hell for eternity? No. Just turn down the music.

Don't get me wrong: All those "Death to America" and "Death to Israel" murals are impossible to justify. But they seemed so incongruous with the gregarious people I met. Do the Iranians literally wish "death" to the US and Israel? Or is it a mix of international road rage, fear, frustration—and the seductive clarity of a catchy slogan?

No Credit Cards, Alcohol...or Urinals

While pondering weighty issues can be thought-provoking, the little everyday differences you encounter while traveling are vividly memorable. As I journeyed through Iran, my notebook filled with quirky observations. One moment, I'd be stirred by propaganda murals encouraging young men to walk into the blazing sunset of martyrdom. The next, a woman in a bookstore served me cookies while I browsed. Then, as I was about to leave without buying anything, she gave me—free of charge—a book I'd admired.

While English is the second language on many signs, and young, well-educated people routinely speak English, communication was often challenging. The majority of Iranians are ethnically Persian. Persians are not Arabs, and they don't speak Arabic—they speak Persian (also called Farsi).

This Persian/Arab difference is a very important distinction to the people of Iran. I heard over and over again, "We are not Arabs!"

In this mural (filling the entire wall of a building), martyrs walk heroically into the sunset of death for God and country.

In a bookstore, a woman patiently showed me fine poetry books. As we left, she gave me a book for free.

The squiggly local script looked like Arabic to me, but I learned that, like the language, it's Farsi. The numbers, however, are the same as those used in the Arab world. Thankfully, when I needed it, I found that they also use the same numbers we do.

Iran is a cash society. Because of the three-decade-old American embargo here, Western credit cards didn't work. No ATMs for foreigners meant that I had to bring in big wads of cash...and learn to count carefully. The money came with lots of zeros. One dollar was equal to 10,000 *rial*.

A *toman* is ten *rial*, and some prices are listed in *rial*, others in *toman*...a tourist rip-off just waiting to happen. I had a shirt laundered at the hotel for "20,000." Was that in *rial* ($2)—or in *toman* ($20)?

People in Iran need to keep track of three different calendars: Persian (for local affairs), Islamic (for religious affairs), and Western (for dealing with the outside world). What's the year? It depends: After the great Persian empire—some 2,500 years ago; after Muhammad—about 1,390 years ago; or after Christ—just over 2,000 years ago.

Of course, the Islamic government legislates women's dress and public behavior (we'll get to that later). Men are also affected, to a lesser degree. Neckties are rarely seen, as they're considered the mark of a Shah supporter. And there seem to be no urinals anywhere. (I did an extensive search—at the airport, swanky hotels, the university, the fanciest coffee shops—and never saw one.) I was told that Muslims believe you don't get rid of all your urine when you urinate standing up. For religious

While Washington made it on our one-dollar bill, Khomeini made it on every denomination in Iran.

reasons, they squat. I found this a bit time-consuming. In a men's room with 10 urinals, a guy knows at a glance what's available; in a men's room with 10 doors, you have to go knocking. (And now I can empathize with women who do this all the time.)

Seyed made sure we ate in comfortable (i.e., high-end) restaurants, generally in hotels. Restaurants used Kleenex rather than napkins; there was a box of tissues on every dining table. Because Iran is a tea culture, the coffee at breakfast was Nescafé-style instant. Locals assured me that tap water was safe to drink, but I stuck with the bottled kind. Iran is strictly "dry"—absolutely no booze or beer in public.

From a productivity point of view, it seemed as if the country were on Valium. Perhaps Iranians are just not driven as we are by capitalist values to "work hard" in order to enjoy material prosperity. I heard that well-employed Iranians made $5,000 to $15,000 a year, and paid essentially no tax. (Taxes are less important to a government funded by oil.) While the Islamic Revolution

Because Iran is "dry," would-be beer-drinkers seem to fantasize. They drink a "malt beverage" that tastes like beer and comes in a beer can, but is non-alcoholic.

is not anti-capitalistic, the business metabolism felt like a communist society: There seemed to be a lack of incentive to really be efficient. Measuring productivity at a glance, things were pretty low-energy.

I couldn't help but think how tourism could boom here if they just opened up. There were a few Western tourists (mostly Germans, French, Brits, and Dutch). All seemed to be on a tour, with a private guide, or visiting relatives. Control gets tighter or looser depending on the political climate, but basically American tourists could visit only with a guided tour. I met no one just exploring on their own. The Lonely Planet guidebook, which is excellent, dominated the scene—it seemed every Westerner in Iran had one. Tourists are so rare, and major tourist sights are so few and obvious, that I bumped into the same travelers day after day. Browsing through picture books and calendars showing the same 15 or 20 images of the top sights in Iran, I was impressed by how our short trip would manage to include most of them.

My travel sensibilities tingling from all these discoveries, I was excited to visit the University of Tehran. There I hoped to find another side of Iran:

highly educated and liberated women and an environment of freedom. I assumed that in Iran, as in most societies, the university would be where people run free...barefoot through the grass of life, leaping over silly limits just because they can.

But instead, the University of Tehran—the country's oldest, biggest, and most prestigious university—made BYU look like Berkeley. Subsidized by the government, the U. of T. followed the theocracy's guidelines to a T: a strictly enforced dress code, no nonconformist posters, top-down direction for ways to play, segregated cafeterias...and students toeing the line (in public, at least).

Hoping to interact with some students, I asked for a student union center (the lively place where students come together as on Western campuses). But there was none. Each faculty had a canteen where kids could hang out, with a sales counter separating two sections—one for boys and one for girls.

In the US, I see university professors as a bastion of free thinking, threatening in a constructive way to people who enjoy the status quo. In Tehran, I found a situation where the theocracy was clearly shaping the curriculum, faculty, and tenor of the campus. Conformity on any university campus saddens me. But seeing it in Iran—a society which so needs some nonconformity—was the most disheartening experience of my entire trip.

Imagine Every Woman's a Nun

My visit to the university jolted me back into the reality of traveling in a society where morality is legislated—where a crime is a sin, and a sin is a crime. In their day-to-day lives, the women of Iran are keenly aware of the impact of living in a theocracy. The days when the Shah's men boasted that miniskirts were shorter in Tehran than they were in Paris are clearly long gone. In the post-Islamic Revolution Iran, modesty rules, and the dress and behavior of women are carefully controlled.

Given the strict dress code, the face is an Iranian woman's powerful tool. If the nose isn't quite right, it can be fixed. We saw many nose jobs healing. And those eyes...truly a contact sport.

While things are casual at home, Iranian women are expected not to show their hair or show off the shape of their body in public. This means that, when out and about, a proper woman covers everything except her face and hands. There are two key components to traditional dress: Hijab ("hih-JOB") means to be dressed modestly, with the head covered under a scarf. The chador ("shah-DORE") is a head-to-toe black cloak wrapped around the front and over the head. All women must follow hijab rules, and many older, rural, and traditional women choose to wear a chador.

In addition to the dress code, Iranian women face other limitations. They're relegated to separate classrooms and sections in mosques. While they are welcome at more genteel sports, they are not allowed to attend soccer games (for fear that they might overhear some foul language from the impassioned fans).

Women can choose to ride in segregated subway cars. Rather than an oppressive measure, this offers a welcome option to sit apart from strange men.

On the subway, women have two options: Ride with men in the mixed cars, or in a separate, women-only car. (When I questioned an Iranian woman about this, she said, "Perhaps the women of New York wished they had a car only for them to avoid the men on their subway trains.")

From a Western viewpoint, it's disrespectful (at best) to impose these regulations on women. But from a strict Muslim perspective, it's the opposite: Mandated modesty is a sign of great respect. In the Islamic Republic of Iran, women's bodies are not vehicles for advertising. Having scantily clad babes selling cars at a trade show would be considered unacceptably disrespectful. You don't see sexy magazines. There is almost no public display of affection. In theory, the dress code provides a public "uniform," allowing men and women to work together without the distractions of sex and flirtation.

Still not buying it? You're not the only one. Local surveys indicate that about 70 percent of these women would dress more freely in public, if allowed. Many push the established bounds of decency—with belts defining the shape

of their bodies and scarves pulled back
to show voluptuous cascades of hair—
when out on the streets. When filming, I found the women's awareness of
our camera fascinating—they seemed
to sense when it was near, and would
adjust their scarves to be sure their hair
was properly covered.

In spite of attempts to enforce
modesty, vanity is not out of bounds.
Women still utilize their feminine
charms. In a land where showing any
cleavage in public is essentially against

Women are covered, yet beautiful...
a wisp of hair can be ravishing.

the law, a tuft of hair above the forehead becomes the exciting place a man's
eye tends to seek out. Cosmetic surgery—especially nose jobs—is big business here among the middle class. Faces are beautifully made up, and—when
so much else is covered—can be particularly expressive and mysterious.
Throughout Iran, I was impressed by the eye contact.

Trying to grasp Iran's mandated modesty in Christian terms, I imagined
living in a society where every woman is forced to dress like a nun. Seeing
spunky young Muslim women chafing at their modesty requirements, I kept
humming, "How do you solve a problem like Maria?"

Iran's "Revolution of Values": Living in a Theocracy

The status of women in Iranian society is just one of many ways in which
Iran's theocracy affects everyday life. For example, as I settled into a plane flying us between two Iranian towns, the pilot announced, "In the name of God
the compassionate and merciful, we welcome you to this flight. Now fasten
your seatbelts." Even though Iran is technically a "Shia democracy" with an
elected president, the top cleric—a man called the "Supreme Leader"—has
the ultimate authority. His picture (not the president's) is everywhere.

The seeds of the Islamic Republic of Iran were sowed during the Islamic
Revolution in 1979. The rebellion, with its spiritual leader Ayatollah Khomeini,
led to the overthrow of the US-backed Shah and the taking of 52 Americans
hostage for 444 days. As a gang of students captured the world's attention
by humiliating the US, this was a great event for the revolutionaries...and
a wrenching one for Americans.

The former US Embassy, where the crisis took place, was a stop on our filming route. Our minder/guide, Seyed, seemed almost proud to let us walk the long wall of anti-American murals. He encouraged us to film it, making sure we knew when the light was best for the camera.

As I walked along the wall, it occurred to me that the crisis had happened three decades ago. While it remains a sore spot for many Americans, Iranians—over half of whom weren't even born at the time—appeared content to let the murals fade in the sun. The murals seemed to drone on like an unwanted call to battle...a call that people I encountered had simply stopped hearing. In fact, looking back, many Iranians believe that the hostage crisis hijacked their Revolution. By radicalizing their country, it put things in the hands of the more hard-line clerics.

Today the Islamic Revolution has become deeply ingrained. After chatting with one young man who didn't look as if he was particularly in compliance with the Revolution, we said goodbye. Later—after he'd thought about our conversation—he returned to tell me, "One present from you to me, please. You must read Quran. Is good. No politics." Looking at the evangelical zeal in his eyes, I realized that he had just as earnest a concern for my soul as a pair of well-dressed Mormons who might stop me on the street back home. Why should a Muslim evangelist be any more surprising (or annoying, or menacing) than a Christian one? He simply cared about me.

Thirty years later, the former US Embassy wall is still lined with hateful political posters.

Seeing the Ayatollah Khomeini from the Iranian perspective was jarring: Rather than the impression I'd long held—of a threatening, unsmiling ideologue— many Iranians consider Khomeini a lovable sage... unpretentious, approachable, and a defender of traditional values. After the Shah's excesses and corruption, locals seemed

Imam Khomeini Revolution Is The Revolution Of Values

For many Iranians, what they would call "family values" trumps democracy and freedom. That's why they follow a supreme leader: Khomeini (right) and his successor Ali Khamenei (left).

to overlook Khomeini's own brutal tactics. Khomeini's simplicity and holiness had a strong appeal to the Iranian masses. Locals told me that Khomeini had charisma, and if he walked into a room, even I, a non-Muslim, would feel it. To the poor and the simple country folk, Khomeini was like a messiah. As the personification of the Islamic Revolution, he symbolized deliverance from the economic and cultural oppression of the Shah. Khomeini gave millions of Iranians hope. Khomeini's successor, Ayatollah Ali Khamenei, has had much less of an impact on the people. (I imagine Shia Muslims miss Khomeini like Catholics miss John Paul II.)

Iranians who support the Revolution call it a "Revolution of Values." Many conservative Iranians I met told me they want to raise their children without cheap sex, disrespectful clothing, drug abuse, and materialism—all things they associate with America, and all things that, they believe, erode character and threaten their traditional values. It worries them as parents. It seemed to me that many of them willingly trade democracy and political freedom for a society free of Western values (or, they'd say, "Western lack of values"). It's more important to them to have a place to raise their children that fits their faith and their cherished notion of "family values." One mother told me, "We don't want our girls to become like Britney Spears."

Of course, there's plenty of drug addiction, materialism, and casual sex in Iran. But these vices are pretty well hidden from the determination of the theocracy to root them out. In general, the Revolution seems to be well-established. For example, in terms of commercialism, Iran and the US stand at opposite extremes. Back home, just about everywhere we look, we are inundated by advertising encouraging us to consume. Airports are paid to drone commercials on loud TVs. Magazines are beefy with slick ads. Sports stars wear corporate logos. Our media are shaped and driven by corporate marketing. But in Iran, Islam reigns. Billboards, Muzak, TV programming, and young people's education all trumpet the teachings of great Shia holy men...at the expense of the economy. Consequently, many in Iranian society tune into Western media via satellites and the Internet, and barely watch Iranian media. Iran's youth are very Web-savvy.

Despite all of this, when it comes to religion, I was surprised by the general mellowness of the atmosphere in Iran compared to other Muslim countries I've visited. Except for the strict women's dress codes and the lack of American products and businesses (because of the US embargo), life on the streets in Iran was much the same as in secular cities elsewhere. In fact, ironically, despite the aggressively theocratic society, the country felt no more spiritual than neighboring, secular Muslim nations. During my visit, I didn't see spiny minarets and didn't hear calls to prayer—a strong contrast to my Ramadan visit to Istanbul the previous year (described in Chapter 6).

While the focus of my trip was on the people rather than the politics, Iran's theocracy makes civil rights concerns unavoidable. Civil liberties for women, religious minorities, and critics of the government are the mark of any modern, free, and sustainable democracy. I believe that, given time and a chance to evolve on their cultural terms, the will of any people ultimately prevails. But in Iran, that time is not yet here. For now, this country is not free. (And no one here claims it is-locals told me, "Iranian democracy: We are given lots of options...and then the government makes the choice for you.") A creepiness that comes with a "big brother" government pervaded the place. Every day during my visit, I wondered how free-minded people cope.

Iranians are constantly reminded that charity is Muhammad-like. With a religious offering box on literally every street corner, extra money is raised for orphanages, schools, and hospitals.

Esfahan's great Imam Mosque is both a tourist attraction and a vibrant place of worship.

While the Islamic Republic of Iran's constitution does not separate mosque and state, it does allow for other religions...with provisions. I asked Seyed if people must be religious here. He said, "In Iran, you can be whatever religion you like, as long as it is not offensive to Islam." Christian? "Sure." Jewish? "Sure." Bahá'i? "No. We believe Muhammad—who came in the seventh century—was the last prophet. The Bahá'i prophet, Bahá'u'lláh, came in the 19th century. Worshipping someone who came after Muhammad is offensive to Muslims. That is why the Bahá'i faith is not allowed in Iran."

I asked, "So Christians and Jews are allowed. But what if you want to get somewhere in the military or government?" Seyed answered, "Then you'd better be a Muslim." I added, "A practicing Shia Muslim?" He said, "Yes."

Friday: Let Us Pray

Esfahan, Iran's "second city" with over 3 million people, is a showcase of ancient Persian splendor. One of the finest cities in Islam, and famous for its dazzling blue-tiled domes and romantic bridges, the city is also just plain enjoyable. I'm not surprised that in Iran, this is the number-one honeymoon destination.

Everything in Esfahan seems to radiate from the grand Imam Square, dominated by the Imam Mosque—one of the holiest in Iran. Dating from the early 1600s, its towering facade is as striking as the grandest cathedrals of Europe.

We were in Iran for just one Friday, the Muslim "Sabbath." Fortunately, we were in Esfahan, so we could attend (and film) a prayer service at this colossal house of worship.

Filming in a mosque filled with thousands of worshippers required permission. Explaining our needs to administrators there, it hit me that the Islamic Revolution employs strategies similar to a communist takeover: Both maintain power by installing partisans in key positions. But the ideology Iran is enforcing is not economic (as it was in the USSR), but religious.

President Ahmadinejad has inspired a fashion trend in Iran: simple dark suit, white shirt, no tie, light black beard. Reminiscent of apparatchiks in Soviet times, it seemed to me that all the mosque administrators dressed the part and looked like the president.

To film the service—which was already well underway—we were escorted in front of 5,000 people praying. When we had visited this huge mosque the day before, all I had seen was a lifeless shell with fine tiles for tourists to photograph. An old man had stood in the center of the floor and demonstrated the haunting echoes created by the perfect construction. Old carpets had been rolled up and were strewn about like dusty cars in a haphazard parking lot. Today the carpets were rolled out, cozy, orderly, and lined with worshippers.

As everyone bowed down in prayer, they revealed soldiers providing security and a "Death to Israel" banner.

I felt self-conscious—a tall, pale American tiptoeing gingerly over the little tablets Shia Muslim men place their heads on when they bend down to pray. Planting our tripod in the corner, we observed.

As my brain wandered (just like it sometimes does at home when listening to a sermon), I felt many of those worshippers were looking at me rather than listening to their cleric speaking. Soldiers were posted throughout the mosque, standing like statues in their desert-colored fatigues. When the congregation stood, I didn't notice them, but when all bowed, the soldiers remained standing—a reminder of the tension within the Islamic world. I asked Seyed to translate a brightly painted banner above the worshippers. He answered, "Death to Israel."

Despite this disturbing detail, I closed my eyes and let the smell of socks remind me of mosques I'd visited in other Muslim countries. I pulled out my little Mecca compass, the only souvenir I'd purchased so far. Sure enough, everyone was facing exactly the right way.

Watching all the worshippers bow and stand, and pray in unison, at first seemed threatening to me. Then I caught the eye of a worshipper having a tough time focusing. He winked. Another man's cell phone rang. He struggled with it as if thinking, "Dang, I should have turned that thing off." The mosaics above— Turkish blue and darker Persian blue—added a harmony and calmness to the atmosphere.

I made a point to view the service as if it were my own church, back in Seattle. I was struck by the similarities: the too-long sermon, responsive readings, lots of getting up and getting down, the "passing of the peace" (when everyone greets the people around them),

After the service, the cleric was eager to talk with us.

the convivial atmosphere as people line up to shake the hand of the cleric after the service, and the fellowship afterwards as everyone hangs out in the courtyard. On our way out, I shook the hand of the young cleric—he had a short, slight build, a tight white turban, a trim Ahmadinejad-style beard, big teeth, and a playful smile. He reminded me of Rafsanjani, Iran's moderate former president. In the courtyard, a man hit the branches of a mulberry tree with a pole as kids scrambled for the treasured little berries.

Esfahan TV, which had televised the prayer service, saw us and wanted an interview. It was exciting to be on local TV. They asked why we were here, how I saw Iranian people, and why I thought there was a problem between the US and Iran. (I pointed out the "Death to Israel" banner, for starters.)

They fixated on whether our show would actually air...and if we'd spin our report to make Iran look evil.

Leaving the mosque, our crew pondered how easily the footage we'd just shot could be cut and edited to appear either menacing or heartwarming, depending on our agenda. Our mosque shots could be juxtaposed with guerillas leaping over barbed wire and accompanied by jihadist music to

be frightening. Instead, we planned to edit it to match our actual experience: showing the guards and "Death to Israel" banner, but focusing on the men with warm faces praying with their sons at their sides, and the children outside scrambling for mulberries.

After prayer service at the mosque, a proud dad grabs a photo of his children.

It occurred to me that the segregation of the sexes—men in the center and women behind a giant hanging carpet at the side—contributes to the negative image many Western Christians have of Islam. Then, playing the old anthropologist's game of changing my perspective, I considered how the predominantly male-led Christian services that I'm so comfortable with could also be edited to look ominous to those unfamiliar with the rituals. At important Roman Catholic Masses, you'll see a dozen priests—all male—in robes before a bowing audience. The leader of a billion Catholics is chosen by a secretive, ritual-filled gathering of old men in strange hats and robes with chanting, incense, and the ceremonial drinking of human blood. It could be filled with majesty, or with menace...depending on what you show and how you show it.

We set up to film across the vast square from the mosque. My lines were memorized and I was ready to go. Then, suddenly, the cleric with the beaming smile came toward us with a platter of desserts—the local ice cream specialty, like frozen shredded wheat sprinkled with coconut. I felt like Rafsanjani himself was serving us ice cream. We had a lively conversation, joking about how it might help if his president went to my town for a prayer service, and my president came here.

Persepolis: Palace of Persia's King of Kings

The sightseeing highlight of our time in Iran was Persepolis. Persepolis was the dazzling ceremonial capital of the Persian Empire, back when it reached from Greece to India. Built by Darius and his son Xerxes the Great around 500 B.C., this sprawling complex of royal palaces was—for nearly two hundred years—the awe-inspiring home of the "King of Kings." At the time, Persia was so mighty, no fortifications were needed. Still, 10,000 guards served at the pleasure of the emperor. Persepolis, which evokes the majesty of Giza or Luxor in Egypt, is (in my opinion) the greatest ancient site between the Holy Land and India.

My main regret from traveling through Iran on my first visit, back in 1978, was not trekking south to Persepolis. And I wanted to include Persepolis in our TV show because it's a powerful reminder that the soul of Iran is Persia, which predates the introduction of Islam by well over a thousand years. Arriving at Persepolis, in the middle of a vast and arid plain, was thrilling. This is one of those rare places that comes with high expectations...and actually exceeds them.

We got to Persepolis after a long day of driving—just in time for that magic hour before the sun set. The light was glorious, the stones glowed rosy, and all the visitors seemed to be enjoying a special "sightseeing high." I saw more Western tourists visiting Persepolis than any other single sight in the

Persepolis is pharaoh-like in its scale. Emperors' tombs are cut into the neighboring mountains.

About 2,500 years ago, subjects of the empire (from 28 nations) would pass in "we're not worthy"-style through the Nations' Gate, bearing gifts for the "King of Kings."

country. But I was struck most by the Iranian people who travel here to savor this reminder that their nation was a mighty empire 2,500 years ago.

Wandering the site, you feel the omnipotence of the Persian Empire and gain a strong appreciation for the enduring strength of this culture and its people. I imagined this place at its zenith: the grand ceremonial headquarters of the Persian Empire. Immense royal tombs, reminiscent of those built for Egyptian pharaohs, are cut into the adjacent mountainside. The tombs of Darius and Xerxes come with huge carved reliefs of ferocious lions. Even today—2,500 years after their deaths—they're reminding us of their great power. But, as history has taught us, no empire lasts forever. In 333 B.C., Persepolis was sacked and burned by Alexander the Great, replacing Persian dominance with Greek culture...and Persepolis has been a ruin ever since.

The approach to this awe-inspiring sight is marred by a vast and ugly tarmac with 1970s-era parking lot light poles. This paved hodgepodge is a reminder of another megalomaniac ruler. In 1971, the Shah threw a bash with unprecedented extravagance to

Iranians—quick to smile for the camera of a new American friend—visit Persepolis to connect with and celebrate their impressive cultural roots.

Tarmac is all that remains of the Shah's big party in 1971.

celebrate the 2,500-year anniversary of the Persian Empire—and to remind the world that he was the latest in a long string of great kings who ruled Persia with the omnipotence of a modern-day Xerxes or Darius. The Shah flew in dignitaries from all over the world, along with dinner from Maxim's in Paris, one of the finest restaurants in Europe. Iranian historians consider this arrogant display of imperial wealth and Western decadence—which so offended his poverty-stricken subjects—the beginning of the end for the Shah. Within a decade, he was gone and Khomeini was in. It's my hunch that the ugly asphalt remains of the Shah's party are left here so visiting locals can remember who their Revolution overthrew.

Martyrs' Cemetery: Countless Deaths for God and Country

I make a point to visit war cemeteries in my travels. They always seem to come with a healthy dose of God—as if dying for God and country makes a soldier's death more meaningful than just dying for country. That is certainly true at Iran's many martyrs' cemeteries.

Most estimates are that there were over a million casualties in the Iran-Iraq War. While the United States lives with the scars of Vietnam, the same generation of Iranians lives with the scars of its war with Iraq—in which they, with one-quarter our population, suffered three times the deaths. Iran considers anyone who dies defending the country to be a hero and a martyr. This bloody conflict left each Iranian city with a vast martyrs' cemetery. Tombs seem to go on forever, and each one has a portrait of the martyr and flies a green, white, and red Iranian flag. All the death dates are from 1980 to 1988.

Could be anywhere: A mother remembers her son—lost for God and country.

Two decades after the war's end, the cemetery was still very much alive with mourning loved ones. A steady wind blew through seas of flags on the day of our visit, which added a stirring quality to the scene. And the place was bustling with people—all mourning their lost loved ones as if the loss happened a year ago rather than twenty. The cemetery had a quiet dignity, and—while I felt a bit awkward at first (being part of an American crew with a big TV camera)—people either ignored us or made us feel welcome.

We met two families sharing a dinner on one tomb (a local tradition). They insisted we join them for a little food and told us their story: They met each other twenty years ago while visiting their martyred sons, who were buried side by side. They became friends, their surviving children married each other, and ever since then they gather regularly to share a meal on the tombs of their sons.

A few yards away, a long row of white tombs stretched into the distance, with only one figure interrupting the visual rhythm created by the receding tombs. It was a mother cloaked in black sitting on her son's tomb, praying—a pyramid of maternal sorrow.

Nearby was a different area: marble slabs without upright stones, flags, or photos. This zone had the greatest concentration of mothers. My friend explained that these slabs marked bodies of unidentified heroes. Mothers whose sons were never found came here to mourn.

I left the cemetery sorting through a jumble of thoughts:

How oceans of blood were shed by both sides in the Iran-Iraq War—a war of aggression waged by Saddam Hussein and Iraq (with American support) against Iran.

How invasion is nothing new for this mighty and historic nation. (When I visited the surprisingly humble National Museum of Archaeology in Tehran, the curator apologized, explaining that the art treasures of his country were scattered in museums throughout Europe and the West.)

How an elderly, aristocratic Iranian woman had crossed the street to look me in the eye and tell me, "We are proud, we are united, and we are strong. When you go home, please tell your people the truth."

How, with a reckless military action, this society could be set ablaze and radicalized. The uniquely Persian mix of delightful shops, university students with lofty career aspirations, gorgeous young adults with groomed eyebrows and perfect nose jobs, hope, progress, hard work, and the gentle people I encountered here in Iran could so easily and quickly be turned into a fiery hell of dysfunctional cities, torn-apart families, wailing mothers, newly empowered clerics, and radicalized people.

How has this boy's loss shaped his worldview?

My visit to the cemetery drove home a feeling that had been percolating throughout my trip. There are many things that Americans justifiably find outrageous about the Iranian government—from supporting Hezbollah, financing Iraqi resistance to the US occupation there, and making threats against Israel; to oppressing women and gay people; to asserting their right to join the world's nuclear club. And yet, no matter how strongly we want to see our demands met by Iran, we must pursue that aim carefully. What if our saber-rattling doesn't coerce this country into compliance? In the past, other powerful nations have underestimated Iran's willingness to be pulverized in a war to defend its ideals...and both Iran and their enemies have paid the price.

I have to believe that smart and determined diplomacy can keep the Iranians—and us—from having to build giant new cemeteries for the next generation's war dead. That doesn't mean "giving in" to Iran...it means acknowledging that war is a failure and we'd be wise to find an alternative.

Back to Europe: Tight Pants, Necklines, Booze... and Freedom

My flight out of Iran was scheduled for 3 a.m. For whatever reason, planes leaving for the West depart in the wee hours. The TV crew had caught an earlier flight, Seyed had gone home, and I was groggy and alone in the terminal.

Finally walking down the jetway toward my Air France plane, I saw busty French flight attendants—hair flowing freely—greeting passengers at the door. It was as if the plane was a lifeboat, and they were pulling us back to the safety of the West. People entered with a sigh of relief, women pulled off their scarves...and suddenly we were free to be what we considered "normal." The jet lifted off, flying the exact opposite route the Ayatollah had traveled to succeed the Shah.

For 12 days, I'd been out of my comfort zone, in a land where people live under a theocracy. I tasted not a drop of alcohol, and I never encountered a urinal. Women were not to show the shape of their body or their hair (and were beautiful nevertheless). It was a land where people took photos of me, as if I were the cultural spectacle.

Landing in Paris was reverse culture shock. I sipped wine like it was heaven-sent. I noticed hair, necklines, and the curves revealed by tight pants like never before. University students sat at outdoor cafés, men and women mingling together as they discussed whatever hot-button issue interested them. After the Valium-paced lifestyle of Iran, I felt an energy and efficiency cranked up on high. People were free to be "evil" and able to express their joy any way they wanted. And, standing before that first urinal, I was thankful to be a Westerner. I was grateful for the learning experience that gave simple things—from visiting the men's room to dealing with traffic jams, from valuing nonconformity to respecting women—a broader cultural context.

Reflecting on My Motives...
and the Real Souvenir I Carried Home

Returning home to the US, I faced a barrage of questions—mainly, "Why did you go to Iran?" Some were skeptical of my motives, accusing me of just trying to make a buck. (As a businessman, I can assure you there was no risk of a profit in this venture.) Reading the comments readers shared on my blog—some of whom railed against me for "naively" acting as a Jane Fonda-type mouthpiece for an enemy that has allegedly bankrolled terrorists—was also thought-provoking. The whole experience made me want to hug people and scream at the same time. It was intensely human.

I didn't go to Iran as a businessman or as a politician. I went as what I am—a travel writer. I went for the same reasons I travel anywhere: to get out of my own culture and learn, to go to a scary place and find it's not so scary, and to bring distant places to people who've yet to go there. To me, understanding people and their lives is what travel is about, no matter where you go.

I have long held that travel can be a powerful force for peace. Travel promotes understanding at the expense of fear. And understanding bridges conflicts between nations. As Americans, we've endured the economic and human cost of war engulfing Iran's neighbor, Iraq. Seeing Iraq's cultural sites destroyed and its kind people being dragged through the ugliness of that

Young couples—regardless of their presidents—share the same basic dreams and aspirations the world over.

war, I wished I'd been able to take my film crew to Baghdad before the war to preserve images of a peacetime Iraq. As our leaders' rhetoric ramped up the possibility of another war—with Iran—I didn't want to miss that chance again. It's human nature to not want to know the people on the receiving end of your "shock and awe"—but to dehumanize these people is wrong. I wanted to put a human face on "collateral damage."

It's not easy finding a middle ground between the "Great Satan" and the "Axis of Evil." Some positions (such as President Ahmadinejad denying the Holocaust) are just plain wrong. But I don't entirely agree with many in my own government, either. Yes, there are evil people in Iran. Yes, the rhetoric and policies of Iran's leaders can be objectionable. But there is so much more to Iran than the negative image drummed into us by our media and our government.

As a traveler, I've often found that the more a culture differs from my own, the more I am struck by its essential humanity.

I left Iran impressed more by what we have in common than by our differences. Most Iranians, like most Americans, simply want a good life and a safe homeland for their loved ones. Just like my country, Iran has one dominant ethnic group and religion that's struggling with issues of diversity and change—liberal versus conservative, modern versus traditional, secular versus religious. As in my own hometown, people of great faith are suspicious of people of no faith or a different faith. Both societies seek a defense against the onslaught of modern materialism that threatens their traditional "family values." Both societies are suspicious of each other, and both are especially suspicious of each other's government.

When we travel—whether to the "Axis of Evil" or just to a place where people yodel when they're happy, or fight bulls to impress the girls, or can't serve breakfast until today's croissants arrive—we enrich our lives and better understand our place on this planet. We undercut groups that sow fear, hatred, and mistrust. People-to-people connections help us learn that we can disagree and still coexist peacefully.

Granted, there's no easy solution, but surely getting to know Iranian culture is a step in the right direction. Hopefully, even the most skeptical will appreciate the humanity of 70 million Iranian people. Our political leaders sometimes make us forget that all of us on this small planet are equally precious children of God. Having been to Iran and meeting its people face-to-face, I feel this more strongly than ever.

Chapter 9
Homecoming

After our whirlwind tour, it's time to wrap up our journey. No matter where you go, the final stop is always the same. And thankfully, home is the best destination of all.

Reverse Culture Shock

Having traveled makes being home feel homier than ever. Part of my re-entry ritual is a good, old-fashioned, American-style breakfast with my family at the local diner. I know just how I like it: eggs—over medium, hash browns—burn 'em on both sides, and toast—sourdough done crispy with marionberry jam. As the waitress tops up my coffee and I snap my sugar packet before ripping it open, I think of how, across this planet, there are thousands of entirely different breakfasts eaten by people just as exacting as I am. And, of all those breakfasts, it's clear that this one is the right one for me. I am home.

Considering all the fun I have traveling, feeling thankful to be home affirms my sense that I'm rooted in the right place. I enjoy the same Olympic Mountains view from my kitchen window that I did as a kid. I look out my office window and still see my junior high school.

While I relish the culture shock of being in an exotic, faraway place, I also enjoy the reverse culture shock of returning to the perfect normalcy of home. As if easing from my traveling lifestyle into my home lifestyle, I still function out of my toiletries kit for a few days before completely unpacking. The simplicity of living out of a single bag slowly succumbs to the complexity of living out of a walk-in closet in a big house with light switches and an entertainment system I've yet to master.

Over time, I willingly fall back into the snappy tempo and daily routine of a busy home life. I do this because I am not fundamentally a vagabond. I love my family, have fun running a business, enjoy the fellowship of the coffee hour after church, and savor my daily stroll across town for coffee. If I had a top hat, I'd tip it to the ladies I pass along the way.

And yet, after every trip, things remain a bit out of whack...but only to me. There's a loneliness in having a mind spinning with images, lessons, and memories that can never adequately be shared—experiences such as finding out why the Salvadoran priest ignores his excommunication, why the Dutch celebrate tolerance, and why the dervish whirls. I enjoy the trip-capping challenge of making sense of the confusion, and splicing what I learned into who I am and what I do.

Travel Changes You

Travel doesn't end when you step off the plane into your familiar home airport. The preceding seven chapters—while ranging far and wide across the globe—all illustrate how travel is rich with learning opportunities, and how the ultimate souvenir is a broader outlook. By incorporating those lessons into my being, I am changed. Any traveler can relate to this: On returning from a major trip, you sense that your friends and co-workers have stayed the same, but you're...different. It's enlightening and unsettling at the same time.

A wonderful by-product of leaving America is gaining a renewed appreciation for our country. When frustrated by overwrought bureaucracies overseas, I'm thankful that it's not a daily part of my life back home. When exasperated by population density, I return home grateful to live in a sparsely populated corner of the world. Traveling, I sample different tempos, schedules, seasoning, business environments, and political systems. Some I like better—others I'm glad don't follow me home.

When I return home from any trip, I realize that I am a part of the *terroir* of my home turf, just as the people who so charm me in distant corners of the world are part of theirs. Those people might visit me here, find it interesting, incorporate a few slices of my lifestyle into theirs, and be just as thankful to fly home. While seeing travel as a political act enables us to challenge our society to do better, it also shows us how much we have to be grateful for, to take responsibility for, and to protect.

In addition to gaining a keen appreciation of how blessed we are, travelers also understand that with these blessings come responsibilities. Protecting the poor, civil rights, and our environment are basic to good global citizenship. Travelers experience lands that have a wide gap between rich and poor, places without basic freedoms an American might take for granted, and regions where neglect has led to ruined environments. Packing that experience home, we can become more compassionate, even (or especially) during difficult times.

Because we've seen the extremes in far-away lands, we can better understand the consequences of continued neglect in our own community.

After a thought-provoking trip, I consume news differently. Since I've wandered through war debris with Alen in Mostar, news footage of any city being devastated by bombs suddenly aches with humanity. My memories of friends stiff with shrapnel, and former parks filled with tombstones, push me toward pacifism. During times of saber-rattling, I fly a peace flag from my office building. A neighbor once asked if I knew how much business I've lost by flying that flag. Because of what I've learned about the human costs of war in places such as Bosnia-Herzegovina, El Salvador, and Iran, it hadn't

Even when this Afghan girl and her mother can no longer see me, I live my life at home knowing the world is watching.

occurred to me to measure the economic costs to my business of speaking out for peace. In fact, it's hard for me to understand how someone could support a war they didn't believe in because it was good for their business.

Mark Twain wrote, "Travel is fatal to prejudice, bigotry, and narrow-mindedness." These wise words can be a rallying cry for all travelers once comfortably back home. When courageous leaders in our community combat small-mindedness and ignorance—whether pastors contending with homophobia in their congregations, employers striving to make a workplace color-blind, or teachers standing up for intellectual and creative freedoms—travelers can stand with them in solidarity.

I strive, not always successfully, to be tolerant. As a comfortable, white, Protestant, suburban American, a warm welcome always awaits me over at the tyranny of the majority. I recognize that intolerance can be a natural state of rest. I'm inspired by lands that have morals but don't moralize…lands that make tolerance a guiding virtue and consider peaceful coexistence a victory. I want to celebrate the diversity in American life by making room for different lifestyles. And I want to help shape an America that employs that viewpoint on a global scale as it works to be a constructive member of the family of nations.

Putting Your Global Perspective into Action at Home

Traveling to learn, you find new passions. Had I not seen shantytowns break out like rashes in Istanbul, I might not have gotten tuned into affordable housing issues in my own community. After observing the pragmatic Dutch and Swiss approach to drug abuse, I chose to speak out on drug law reform with NORML and the ACLU. Having traveled in the Islamic Republic of Iran, where religion and government are thoroughly interwoven, I've seen the troubling consequences of mixing mosque or church and state. In my church, some want the American flag right up there in front, while others in my community would like to hang the Ten Commandments in our city hall. And, because I care both for my church and my state, I work to keep my church free of flags and my city hall free of religious commandments.

Travel becomes a political act only if you actually do something with your broadened perspective once you return home. The challenges on the horizon today can be so overwhelming that they freeze caring people into inaction. While trying to save the planet singlehandedly can be disheartening, taking a few concrete and realistic baby steps in that direction can be empowering and bring fine rewards. Because of my work, I've had some exciting opportunities in this regard. Below are a few personal examples of how I've incorporated passions sparked by my travels into real action back home. I'm sharing these in the hopes of demonstrating a few creative ways that you may do the same—on a larger or smaller scale. Here are some concrete ways you can bring your new global perspective into your local citizenship:

Be an advocate for those outside of the US who have no voice here, but are affected by our policies. See our government policy through a lens of how will this impact the poor. Travel forces voters to consider a new twist on "representative" democracy. Whom should your vote represent? Because I've made friends throughout the developing world, my vote is

Once you've met these girls living on a garbage dump in El Salvador, it's hard not to take them along when you enter the voting booth.

based on more than simply, "Am I better off today than I was four years ago?" Travelers recognize that the results of an election here in the US can have a greater impact on poor people half a world away than it does on middle-class American voters. My travels have taught me that you don't want to be really rich in a terribly poor world. With this in mind, I think of it not as noble or heroic, but simply pragmatic to bring a compassion for the needy along with me into the voting booth. I like to say (naively, I know) that if every American were required to travel abroad before voting, the US would fit more comfortably into this ever-smaller planet.

Share lessons, expect more from your friends, and don't be afraid to ruin dinners by bringing up uncomfortable realities. In a land where the afflicted and the comfortable are kept in different corners, people who connect those two worlds are doing everyone a service. Afflict the comfortable in order to comfort the afflicted. By saying things that upset people so they can declare they'd fight and die for my right to be so stupid, I feel I'm contributing to the fabric of our democracy.

Get involved. After observing alarming trends in other countries, it's easier to extrapolate and appreciate where small developments in our own society may ultimately lead—whether it's the impact of a widening gap between rich and poor, a violation of the separation of church and state, the acceptance of

My daughter Jackie's high school trip—a month in a Moroccan village—was her most eye-opening experience yet in life. A trip like that doesn't happen without parents and teachers who appreciate the value of sending students abroad.

a tyranny of the majority, or the loss of personal freedoms. Then, for the good of your community, you understand the importance of becoming active and speaking out to help nip those trends in the bud.

Encourage others to travel. For example, support student exchange programs. Many people have the resources to travel, but live within a social circle where "travel" means Las Vegas and Walt Disney World. High schools and universities are putting more priority than ever on foreign study programs. For many, the funding is a challenge. One trip can help forever broaden the perspective of a young person with a big future. Hosting a foreign student can help create the same amount of international understanding as funding an American student's trip abroad.

Do a survey of causes you might become involved in, choose a couple that resonate, then tackle these as a hobby. Working on my favorites—debt relief for the developing world, drug policy reform, and affordable housing—brings me great joy. I have an excuse to focus my studies, I meet inspirational people, and I enjoy the gratification that comes with actually making a difference. Organizations like Jubilee USA Network need grassroots help in reaching their goal of relief for the world's most heavily indebted nations (www.jubileeusa.org). Look into Bread for the World, a Christian citizens' organization that effectively lobbies our government in the interest of poor and hungry people both in our country and overseas (www.bread.org). If you're inspired to advocate for smarter US drug laws, join NORML (www.norml.org) and talk about it in polite company. There are a host of good organizations and a world of worthy causes to support.

Promote the wisdom and importance of talking to your "enemies," even in everyday life. Confront problems—at home, at work, in your community—with calm, rational, and respectful communication. Support politicians who do the same with foreign policy. France and Germany still mix like wine and sauerkraut, but they've learned that an eternity of agreeing to disagree beats an eternity of violent conflict.

Reach and preach beyond the choir. Don't hold back in places where progressive thinking may seem unwelcome. I was tempted to move to a church downtown that welcomed progressive thinkers, but chose instead to keep sharing a pew with a more conservative gang at my suburban church. Rather than change churches, I've stayed and contributed: teaching poverty awareness workshops, sharing my travels at special events, and—after learning that many in our congregation are homophobic—even inviting the Seattle Men's Chorus (America's largest gay chorus) to provide music one Sunday. While conservatives and liberals may see things differently, they care equally. I've found that, deep down, any thinking person wants to be challenged respectfully and thoughtfully. (That's why, rather than install a new air-conditioning system for our chapel, we built a well in a thirsty Nicaraguan village.)

Travel inside the United States to appreciate the full diversity of culture and thought within our vast, multifaceted society. Tune in to both ethnic diversity and economic diversity. Assume that subcultures—even scary ones—provide basic human necessities. At home and abroad, the vast majority of people who look scary aren't. I remember the first time I walked through Seattle's Hempfest—a party of 80,000 far-out people filling a park. A man named Vivian wearing a Utilikilt and dreadlocks yelled, "Give it up!" for a band whose music sounded like noise to me...and people went wild. It was intimidating. Then I got to know Vivian, who explained to me that this is a subculture that once a year gets to

THINK MULTILATERALLY

Promote multilateralism. Join your local chapter of the UN. In the lead-up to the Iraq War, I designed bumper stickers with the blue-and-white UN flag that said simply "Think Multilaterally" so my neighbors and I could fly our flag without implying we supported a unilateral foreign policy.

come together here on Seattle's waterfront. I walked through the crowd again, with a different attitude. I celebrated the freedom and tolerance that made that tribal gathering possible. Last year I noticed I got strangely emotional when talking with police who said they enjoy the Hempfest assignment as a two-way celebration of respect and tolerance.

Take your broader outlook to work. Until we have "cost accounting" that honestly considers all costs, there is no real financial incentive for corporations to consider the environment, the fabric of our communities, the poor at home or abroad, or our future in their decisions. Executives are legally required to maximize profits, but with leadership and encouragement coming from their workforce, they are more likely to be good citizens as well as good businessmen. I encourage my employees to guard my travel company's ethics and stand up to me if I stray. And they do.

Remember that many would love to travel and gain a broader perspective, but cannot. Find creative ways to bring home the value of travel by giving presentations to groups of curious people not likely to have passports. I did this back in my twenties by hosting a monthly "World Travelers' Slide Club," and do essentially the same thing on a bigger scale today by producing a radio show that I offer free each week to our nation's network of public radio stations.

Consider an educational tour for your next trip (see, for example, Augsburg College's Center for Global Education, www.augsburg.edu/global). Even if you normally wouldn't take a tour, visiting trouble zones with a well-connected organization is safe, makes you an insider, and greatly increases your opportunities for learning. I've taken three such tours, and each has

been powerfully educational and inspirational. Educational tourism is a small yet thriving part of the tourism industry and offers a world of options.

Seek out balanced journalism. Assume commercial news is entertainment—it thrives on making storms (whether

Educational tours build in time to share and reflect.

political, military, terrorist-related, or actual bad weather) as exciting as they can get away with in order to increase their audience so they can charge more for advertising. Money propels virtually all media. Realize any information that comes to you has an agenda. If you're already consuming lots of TV news, read a progressive alternative source that's not so corporation-friendly (such as *The Nation* magazine, www.thenation.com).

Conquering fear and ethnocentrism through world exploration rewards the traveler with a grand and global perspective.

Read books that explain the economic and political basis of issues you've stumbled onto in your travels. A basic understanding of the economics of poverty, the politics of empire, and the power of corporations are life skills that give you a foundation to better understand what you experience in your travels. Information that mainstream media considers "subversive" won't come to you. You need to reach out for it. The following are a few of the books (listed in chronological order) that have shaped and inspired my thinking over the years: *Bread for the World* (Arthur Simon), *Food First* (Frances Moore Lappé), *The Origins of Totalitarianism* (Hannah Arendt), *Future in Our Hands* (Erik Dammann), *Manufacturing Consent* (Noam Chomsky), *War Against the Poor: Low-Intensity Conflict and Christian Faith* (Jack Nelson-Pallmeyer), *Unexpected News: Reading the Bible with Third World Eyes* (Robert McAfee Brown), *The United States of Europe* (T. R. Reid), *The European Dream* (Jeremy Rifkin), and *The End of Poverty* (Jeffrey Sachs).

Find ways to translate your new global passions to local needs. Like the bumper sticker says: Think globally…act locally. Travel has taught me the reality of homelessness. Talking with a proud and noble woman like Beatriz in El Salvador—which does more to humanize the reality of poverty than reading a library of great books on the subject—inspires you to action once back home. Thinking creatively, my wife and I used our retirement savings to purchase a small apartment complex that we loaned to the YWCA to use to house local homeless mothers. Now, rather than collect taxable interest, we climb into our warm and secure bed each night knowing that 25 struggling moms and their kids do as well. When you can learn to vicariously enjoy the consumption of someone who's dealing with more basic needs than you are, you are richer for it. With this outlook, helping to provide housing to people in need is simply smarter, more practical, and more gratifying than owning a big yacht. (This can be done on a smaller scale with much less equity, too. For more details, see www.ricksteves.com/politicalact.)

Find creative ways to humanize our planet while comfortably nestled into your workaday home life. Sweat with the tropics, see developing-world debt as the slavery of the 21st century, and feel the pain of "enemy losses" along with the pain of American losses. Do things—even if only symbolic—in solidarity with people on the front lines of struggles you care about.

Put your money where your ideals are. Know your options for local consumption and personal responsibility. Don't be bullied by non-sustainable cultural norms. You can pay more for your bread to buy it from the person who baked it. You can buy seasonal produce in a way that supports family farms. You can, as a matter of principle, shun things you don't want to support (bottled water, disposable goods, sweatshop imports, and so on). You can use public transit or drive a greener car. Consume as if your patronage helps shape our future. It does.

Participate in the Travel as a Political Act Readers' Forum at my website (www.ricksteves.com/politicalact). It's designed so that we travelers can share ideas and encourage and inspire each other. Please join the discussion there, share thoughts generated by this book, and contribute ways you've enjoyed incorporating your worldview into your local activism.

Keep on Whirling

With the fall of the USSR, I remember thinking, "Wow, the USA will reign supreme on this planet through the rest of my lifetime." It seemed that American values of democracy and the free market would be unstoppable. And American economic might, coupled with our hardball approach to maintaining our relative affluence, would be insurmountable. We would just keep getting richer and more powerful.

Of course, the outlook today is more sober. We've been humbled by the consequences of our isolation, the limits of our military power, the collapse of the housing and stock markets, the costly specter of global warming, and the meteoric rise of India and China as economic giants.

In this Global Age, the world's problems are *our* problems. It'll be all hands on deck. We need to address these challenges honestly and wisely. Lessons learned from our travels can better equip us to address and help resolve the challenges facing our world. We travelers are both America's ambassadors to the world...and the world's ambassadors to America.

Whether you're a mom, a schoolteacher, a celebrity, a realtor, or a travel writer, it's wrong to stop paying attention and let others (generally with a vested interest in the situation) make political decisions for us. Our founding fathers didn't envision career politicians and professional talking heads doing our political thinking for us. All are welcome in the political discourse that guides this nation.

Thoughtful travelers know that we're all citizens of the world and members of a global family. Spinning from Scotland to Sri Lanka, from Tacoma to Tehran, travelers experience the world like whirling dervishes: We keep one foot planted in our homeland, while acknowledging the diversity of our vast world. We celebrate the abundant and good life we've been given and work to help those blessings shower more equitably upon all.

Acknowledgments

I'm grateful to work with people at my company who share my vision and commitment. Many thanks to my editors, Cameron Hewitt and Risa Laib, for bringing clarity, depth, and focus to my writing. If this book has struck a chord with you, it's due largely to their tuning—and even downright overhauling—of my work. Thanks to Rhonda Pelikan for laying out the book so thoughtfully. I also appreciate the talented help of Gene Openshaw, Barb Geisler, Laura VanDeventer, and Lauren Mills. Thanks to my wife, Anne and children, Andy and Jackie, for their patience and support.

I had experts in various fields and from various countries review the portions of my work that relate to their area of expertise. For their insightful guidance, my thanks to Marijan Krišković (tour guide, on the former Yugoslavia), Dr. Benjamin Curtis (Professor, Seattle University, on the European Union), Francesca Caruso (licensed Italian guide, on the EU), Edit Herczog (member of the European Parliament, on the EU), Lee Evans (tour guide and Berlin local, on the EU), Ann Butwell (Center for Global Education at Augsburg College, on El Salvador), Christian Donatzky (Historian, MA, Copenhagen History Tours, on Denmark), Jane Klausen (insider's look at Denmark), David Hoerlein (tour guide, on Denmark), Jakob Nielsen (Danish journalist, on Denmark), Lale Surmen Aran (tour guide and author, on Turkey), Tankut Aran (tour guide and author, on Turkey), Mehlika Seval (tour guide, on Turkey), Aziz Begdouri (tour guide, on Morocco), Norm Stamper (former Seattle Police Chief, on drug policy), Dr. Craig Reinarman (Professor of Sociology, UC Santa Cruz, on drug policy), and Abdi Sami (Associate Producer of *Rick Steves' Iran* public television show).

Thanks to the people mentioned in the anecdotes in this book for giving such meaning and wonder to my travels and my life. And finally, thanks to you, my thoughtful reader, for knowing that travel can—and should be—a positive force for change. Happy travels!

Index

This big-picture index is designed to point you to some of my favorite themes, topics, and destinations. The page numbers direct you only to the main discussion of the item (not each passing mention). The list, shaped by my own preferences, is not comprehensive and admittedly quirky…just like each traveler's own journey.

Public Television:
Rick Steves' Europe

Rick's award-winning travel series has become a public television institution, appearing for the past decade on more than 300 stations nationwide. Every

Rick Steves' Europe episode gives viewers a chance to experience Europe's most interesting destinations, from its great cities to its "back door" hideaways and villages. Because many stations air the shows in high-definition—from the windswept coast of Scotland to the scalps of the Alps to the markets of Istanbul—watching *Rick Steves' Europe* is the next best thing to a plane ticket. All eighty *Rick Steves' Europe* shows are also available as a DVD box set. For details on all of Rick's TV shows, visit ricksteves.com.

Public Radio:
Travel with Rick Steves

Every week Rick Steves, his guest experts and callers share a lively, ear-opening hour of travel talk that connects public radio listeners with the sights, sounds, and cultures of the world. Going far beyond Rick's "home base" of Europe, *Travel with Rick Steves* explores global topics, such as encounters with Islam, bicycle adventures in Asia, ecotourism in Latin America, road trips in the USA, local cooking, cultural quirks, travel as a force for peace, and much more. The show is broadcast by more than 130 radio stations nationwide, and available from anywhere as free podcasts. For a complete list of stations and archived shows, visit ricksteves.com/radio.

Free Travel Podcasts

Rick Steves has built a rich archive of radio shows and "Travel Bites" TV clips that can be played any time, on demand, for free. They are easy to subscribe to and download via iTunes or at ricksteves.com.

Free Audio Tours

Now you can visit Europe's great sights with Rick Steves literally whispering in your ear—making art and history come alive at that very moment. Rick has recorded 16 Audio Tours covering key sights and neighborhood walks in Paris, Rome, Florence, and Venice. All are available free from iTunes and at ricksteves.com. Each tour also includes a handy PDF companion map.

ricksteves.com

Rick Steves' Europe Through the Back Door travel company provides a number of services for travelers heading to Europe. The gateway to all of this is ricksteves.com, which features an extensive plan-your-trip section, daily European headlines for travelers, free access to podcasts, updates for Rick's guidebooks, and deals on railpasses, tours, and travel gear.

European Tours

Rick Steves' tour program offers one- to three-week adventures covering 35 different European itineraries, with "great guides, small groups, and no grumps." If you are looking for an energetic way to travel with free-spirited people in the Rick Steves style, you can learn all the details—and request a free tour catalog and *Rick Steves' Tour Experience* DVD—at ricksteves.com.

Travel Gear

Rick's mantra is "pack light, pack light, pack light." In keeping with this less-is-more philosophy, Rick Steves has created his own value-priced line of carry-on travel bags and accessories, in addition to his guidebooks, maps, and DVDs. They can all be found at the Rick Steves Travel Store at ricksteves.com.

Railpasses

For 50 years, Eurail Passes have given Americans an affordable passport to European adventures. But as the array of

Rick Steves' travel-savvy staff is eager to help you turn your travel dreams into affordable reality.

passes has grown more confusing, it's more important than ever for travelers to get the information they need to make the best choice for their trip. The Eurail Passes section at ricksteves.com does just that, and offers lots of valuable, trip-improving extras with every railpass purchase.

Travel News

Each month Rick sends an on-the-road email dispatch to his 250,000 Travel News subscribers, including a collection of timely travel articles. It's free, and easy to subscribe at ricksteves.com.

Graffiti Wall and Helpline

Don't rely exclusively on Rick's advice—the community corner at ricksteves.com is a great place to look up budget travel advice from thousands of other travelers, and even correspond over particular travel questions you may have.

Other Books by Rick Steves

Rick Steves' Europe Through the Back Door
Rick Steves' Europe 101: History and Art for the Traveler
Rick Steves' Postcards from Europe
Rick Steves' European Christmas

Country Guides
Rick Steves' Best of Europe
Rick Steves' Croatia & Slovenia
Rick Steves' Eastern Europe
Rick Steves' England
Rick Steves' France
Rick Steves' Germany
Rick Steves' Great Britain
Rick Steves' Ireland
Rick Steves' Italy
Rick Steves' Portugal
Rick Steves' Scandinavia
Rick Steves' Spain
Rick Steves' Switzerland

City and Regional Guides
Rick Steves' Amsterdam, Bruges & Brussels
Rick Steves' Athens & the Peloponnese
Rick Steves' Budapest
Rick Steves' Florence & Tuscany
Rick Steves' Istanbul
Rick Steves' London
Rick Steves' Paris
Rick Steves' Prague & the Czech Republic
Rick Steves' Provence & the French Riviera
Rick Steves' Rome
Rick Steves' Venice
Rick Steves' Vienna, Salzburg & Tirol

Phrase Books
Rick Steves' French, Italian & German Phrase Book
Rick Steves' French Phrase Book & Dictionary
Rick Steves' German Phrase Book & Dictionary
Rick Steves' Italian Phrase Book & Dictionary
Rick Steves' Portuguese Phrase Book & Dictionary
Rick Steves' Spanish Phrase Book & Dictionary

Travel as a Political Act Online

www.ricksteves.com/politicalact
To give this book an online life, more depth, and interactivity, we're hosting a "Travel as a Political Act" corner of our website. Here you'll find more information about topics covered in this book, including streaming video of Rick's lectures, a script and related information for the *Rick Steves' Iran* public television special, essays and videos about drug policy reform, blogs and rough journals from trips that inspired chapters in this book, and more. You'll also learn about worthwhile causes that Rick is personally involved in and passionate about. Most importantly, the site features a forum where readers can share their own experiences traveling as a political act. Please join the conversation at www.ricksteves.com/politicalact.

About the Author

Rick Steves, born in 1955 and raised in Edmonds, Washington (just north of Seattle), still looks out his window each morning at Puget Sound. He and his wife, Anne, have raised two children, Andy and Jackie. Rick ventured to Europe for the first time as a teenager in 1969, visiting relatives in Norway and touring German piano factories with his piano-importer father. Rick was hooked...and ever since, he's spent four months each year overseas. After a few trips of learning from his mistakes, Rick was inspired to teach his fellow travelers how to enjoy smoother and

more culturally broadening travels. What began as a series of lectures evolved into guidebooks, guided tours, a public television series (*Rick Steves' Europe*), a public radio show (*Travel with Rick Steves*), a website (ricksteves.com), and a syndicated newspaper column. Rick wrote his first book, *Europe Through the Back Door*, in 1980. Since then, he has researched and written 35 different European travel guidebooks (all published by Avalon Travel Publishing). His Edmonds-based travel company, Rick Steves' Europe Through the Back Door, employs a hardworking and well-traveled staff of 70. An active Lutheran, Rick has hosted several educational videos for the Lutheran Church (ELCA) and received the Wittenberg Award in 2007 for his social activism. In 2009, the National Council for International Visitors (funded by the US State Department) presented Rick with their Citizen Diplomat of the Year Award. Rick still spends four months a year in Europe updating his guidebooks, researching new ones, and producing TV shows, as he has for three decades.